Diary of a Deputy

Diary of a Deputy is a practical guide to deputy headship for busy career teachers. Susan Tranter draws on her own experience of the job to guide aspiring and newly appointed deputy heads through the transition from middle management to school leadership. Each chapter opens with a typical deputy head's daily page, and goes on to offer realistic advice on how to successfully manage different aspects of this complex job. The key areas covered are:

- Why do you want to become a deputy?
- Negotiating the selection process
- Starting the job – the first few weeks
- The task of recruiting new staff
- Teamwork and the role of the deputy
- Being a reflective practitioner
- Balancing your workload
- Leading strategic change

Diary of a Deputy encourages readers to form their own opinions on the issues raised with action points and references to further reading. This is an optimistic yet down-to-earth book that will support and inspire all deputies-to-be.

Susan M. Tranter is Deputy Headteacher at Matthew Arnold School, Oxford.

Diary of a Deputy

Susan M. Tranter

London and New York

First published 2002 by RoutledgeFalmer
11 New Fetter Lane, London EC4P 4EE

Simultaneously published in the USA and Canada
by RoutledgeFalmer
29 West 35th Street, New York, NY 10001

RoutledgeFalmer is an imprint of the Taylor & Francis Group

Cover photograph reproduced by
kind permission of John Cassidy

Typeset in Sabon by
Keystroke, Jacaranda Lodge, Wolverhampton
Printed and bound in Great Britain by
TJ International Ltd, Padstow, Cornwall

British Library Cataloguing in Publication Data
A catalogue record for this book is available from the British Library

Library of Congress Cataloging in Publication Data
Tranter, Susan.
  Diary of a deputy / Susan M. Tranter.
    p. cm.
  Includes bibliographical references and index.
  1. Assistant school principals—Great Britain—Handbooks, manuals, etc.
  2. School management and organization—Great Britain—Handbooks,
  manuals, etc. I. Title.

  LB2831.926.G7 T73 2001
  371.2'012'0941—dc21

                                                          2001034996

ISBN 0–415–24220–7

Contents

Foreword		vi
Introduction		vii
1	So you want to be a deputy?	1
2	Dear Headteacher, Thank you for inviting me for interview	27
3	Starting out	57
4	Assessing the motivated: issues over recruitment?	75
5	Is the honeymoon over?	99
6	If you are going to get better, you have to learn more	129
7	Too much to do?	158
	Epilogue: reflections on a year in the life of . . .	185

Foreword

This book was written during my first year as deputy headteacher at the Matthew Arnold School in Oxford.

When the book was originally conceived, my intention was to write about all that happened during that first year. What has in fact emerged is a set of reflections on the major issues that face school leaders in general, and deputy heads in particular. The incidents in this book and the conversations, are all real, but unless I make specific reference to Matthew Arnold School, no inference should be made. This is in order to protect my colleagues.

This book is dedicated to the headteacher, his staff and the students of Matthew Arnold School.

Introduction

Contracts and conditions of service
There is no specific law governing the terms of contracts of people employed to work in schools . . . The matters that statute requires to be included are:
. . . – full-time teachers (other than headteachers and deputy headteachers) are required to work 195 days a year . . .
. . . – teachers cannot be required to undertake lunchtime supervision and are entitled to a reasonable midday break . . . Headteachers and deputy headteachers have no specified hours or days of work, but are entitled to a midday break.

(Gold and Szemerenyi 1998)

What is a deputy headteacher? The epigraph above expresses the job simply in terms of the conditions of service and the entitlement to a midday break. However, it also makes a distinction between the headteacher and deputy, on the one hand, and the rest of the teaching staff of the school on the other. The conditions of service are different because in a very real sense the job of deputy head-teacher is extremely far removed from the task of teaching classes, leading a subject team or managing the welfare of a student group.

This book is a journey. It starts from my desire to be a deputy headteacher and explores the issues that arose during the first year of my transition from middle manager to school leader. The use of the terms 'manager' and 'leader' are problematic and this theme is explored at various times in this book.

The world of education is changing substantially, and I am by no means the first to point this out. However, the changing nature of society and the concomitant accommodation and assimilation of its ideals makes the world an exciting and vibrant place.

Leading a school is a complex task. It is less about processes and more about communication. Devising elegant and sophisticated systems that identify underachievement and set targets are all very well, but if the people at the 'chalk face' fail to engage with them, then what next? Similarly, the pressures on the education service to provide for the country's future needs are such as to leave no room for complacency.

The ideas that are developed in this book and the issues addressed tell only part of the story. Being a deputy head is not only about strategic leadership. It is about being the person who stays till the end at parents evening. In one day during the period covered by this book I did the following:

- set out chairs in the hall to be ready for the Year 6 induction day (with the head)
- put out a Welcome booklet on every chair
- had a chat with a newly qualified teacher on her first day
- spoke to a parent who was worried about her son's progress
- applied a plaster to a grazed knee
- investigated an incident where a child had been rude to a teacher
- visited the park at lunchtime
- discussed the timetable with a curriculum leader
- photocopied a memo for the entire staff because the resources technician was unwell and had to go home
- comforted a distressed child
- taught two lessons
- discussed capitation with the head
- planned the next senior team meeting
- made tea for the governors' meeting
- photocopied a calendar for someone who'd lost theirs
- gave a presentation to the governors on the school's PANDA (performance and attainment report)
- cleared the cups and plates

This was a busy day but my purpose here is not to emphasise the breadth of responsibility and the occasionally frantic nature of the job. It is more to show how varied the job can be: it is never the same. It brings a real sense that there are things that need to be done to make other things happen, and sometimes the head and deputy are the people who do them. If the chairs need to be cleared away and time is short, then we help the caretaker do the job, because we want to help and there's no one else to do it.

The job presents challenges, and this book seeks to ask questions and enable readers to think through the issues for themselves. It relies on a mixture of theory and reflective practice. Throughout the book there are references to further reading – this is an important part of the work that has gone into this book. In addition, there are summaries and action points at the end of chapters.

A dominant theme that pervades the text is my belief that the work we do to move a school forward makes the world a better place. It creates life chances for those on whom the future of society depends.

Reference

Gold R. and Szemerenyi S. (1998) *Running a School 1998: Legal Duties and Responsibilities* Jordans, Bristol

1   So you want to be a deputy?

Sunday, 15 September [some years ago]

September 15

Things to do today:

1   Go through the timetable for tomorrow.
2   Plan lessons for Years 7, 9, 10, 11, 13 for the week.
3   Think about how to produce work for the display on Open Day.
4   Write names of form group into the register.
5   PSE lesson – record BBC2 7pm programme on attitudes to authority.

Term is now just two weeks old and I'm getting back to work with gusto. My Year 10 class is one that will need a lot of work. The school gave them the NFER Cognitive Ability Tests when they were in Year 7 and so I have a good idea of their overall ability and their target grades. I will need to find out their key stage 3 results, though, to see how much progress they will need to make over the next two years.

In terms of my own progress, then, there are a number of things that I need to think about. I talked to the deputy head about his job today and he gave me some really exciting things to consider. I'm really interested in how to make my teaching better. I don't think that you can lead a school unless you are very good teacher. He suggested that looking at the OfSTED criteria for lesson judgements would be a good way forward.

But if I'm going to be a headteacher in the future I shall have to plan out my career. I'm going to have to think about what skills and experiences I need to acquire. I know that timetable construction is something that deputy heads do – and Joe said that I could get involved this year.

I'm a bit bothered by the school's behaviour policy too. I think that it's not really working any more and that some of the rules that are listed aren't followed. Some of the children don't seem to realise that we have a behaviour policy! I think I'll make an appointment to see the head and suggest that I do some work on this.

Acquiring skills and experiences

The motivation for a senior management role varies considerably from person to person. For some, it will be the exercise of power. Others will be motivated by the need for self-fulfilment. Yet others will find themselves in this position as a result of a sudden opportunity or serendipity. The complex subject of individual motivation will be explored later in this chapter, but attention is drawn to this issue at the outset because thought and careful planning are needed if you are to move to a senior management role. It will not just happen without consideration and an appreciation of what the role involves.

The first requirement, of course, is to be an excellent teacher. Most deputy headteachers will at some time, have the responsibility for ensuring the quality of their school's teaching and learning. It is important therefore to be an excellent teacher yourself. Over recent years, there has been an acknowledgement that teaching is a skill to be acquired, practised and improved. The OfSTED criteria for the assessment of the quality of teaching and learning are sufficiently differentiated to enable you to discriminate between good, very good and excellent teaching. It is possible to identify what you need to do to improve the quality of your teaching. Indeed the target-setting agenda has brought this to the fore. By having targets for our classes, we can show to what extent we add value to those in our charge. It is necessary, however, to be able to prove that you are an excellent teacher; the Threshold Assessment process has illustrated the need for teachers to keep records of their students' achievements; by recording targets and outcomes, you can prove your claim to excellence.

Much of the preparation for senior management, however, is rooted in the need to acquire skills and experience. Many of these can only be acquired over time and with significant and substantial commitment to the cause. For some people, the path to career success is easy and unencumbered. For most of us, there will be frustrations and some measure of disappointment along the way; having a vision, clarity of purpose, and developing a sense of self-belief are the keys to unlock the door to success.

Personal motivation

It is perhaps fortunate that no one has found out what motivates a person. If there were only one thing, then it would, no doubt, be a deficiency model, for all human beings differ. The strength of the human race lies as much in the fact that human motivation has layers of complexity as in its weakness. This means that the panacea for organisational reform collapses under the strain of disparate needs and motives.

The location of motivation as an organisational trait will be explored elsewhere. Here, I discuss what motivates us, as individuals, to strive and to succeed. Handy (1981) describes a hermit in his mountain cell confronted with a Sunday newspaper which makes him wonder why people are doing all the things they do. Certainly, when you look around any organisation or any cultural unit, you may wonder why and how people do what they do.

The question arises of to what extent this is a modern phenomenon. Can we assess the level at which the organisational pressures on schools are the independent variable which determines an individual's motivation? Of course human motivation is far more complicated. However, to address this issue more fully, it is necessary to consider the elements that make up the body of people who call themselves 'teachers'.

What motivates someone to become a teacher? Having surveyed a number of people in my immediate domain, the reasons why people enter the teaching profession are as varied as the subjects they teach. For some, it is a desire to 'tell people what they know'. For others, it is because 'my parents were both teachers'. For many, it was a job they settled for after graduation and never left. The idea of a lifelong career is very strong in teaching; there are those who leave the profession to pursue other opportunities; some go on to fame and great success. But for many, the career they enter in those early years is the one they stay with. Once in the profession, the cultural dimension of education takes a hold. A significant part of any person's development and progression to adulthood is their own education. The influence this brings to bear on the way you teach cannot be overstated. Much of the talk that goes on in school staffrooms is peppered with anecdotes and reflections on individual experience. This is often where teachers let themselves down as a professional body. The anecdotal assertions are just that; they lack any analysis and their value lies in their ability to support a particular point rather than prove a case. As an aspirant teacher, you must learn to transcend personal experience and to root your opinion in that which is more reasoned and supported by research.

You may be motivated by the subject you teach. Teachers often want to tell people about their subject, sharing their enthusiasm for their curriculum area. This can be a strong motivator, but for a deputy headteacher, the influence of your subject is considerably weakened. You are unlikely to be appointed because of a particular subject expertise. It is, of course, one factor: it is vital in an all-graduate entry profession, that the people who lead the school should be intellectually and academically able. However, this point is made to remind you of the need to find ways of building up knowledge of all curriculum areas. Reading the National Curriculum requirements and programmes of study is a good place to start, but informed discussion with your peers is perhaps a better means to find out about each curriculum area.

There has been considerable debate over the status of teaching as a profession. The campaign 'Everybody remembers a good teacher', in which celebrities described their best teacher to the delight of television and cinema audiences, the teacher 'Oscars' and the like have all have been about improving the status of teaching as a profession. That the organisers of such campaigns have, perhaps, had a brief to improve recruitment into the profession does not compromise the aims of the campaign. In any case, the fact remains that there have been concerns about the status of the schoolteacher.

Too often, teachers have been regarded as those who actively prevent change rather than those who cultivate it in order to raise the standards of attainment in schools. The image of the 'high-flier' is difficult for many in teaching to appreciate. However, there are those who want to succeed and get there quickly. They are often the 'movers and shakers' who will want to enjoy rapid success and all that it brings. In a consumer-driven society, the lure of the pound is considerable. For those whose motives differ, there is no hiding place for anyone wanting a quiet life. The sheer quantity of educational change that has occurred over the past twenty years is testament to that. The means now exist to assess children's cognitive ability and to set targets for children and their teachers. The country cannot afford to have an underclass of people who have failed at school, and school leaders have the task of ensuring that the teachers in their school deliver. The pressure on us all is to succeed, to acquire, and to be seen to be a success.

But personal motivation is more complicated than that. Aristotle (384–322 BC) wrote:

> All men seek one goal; success or happiness. The only way to achieve true success is to express yourself completely in service to society. First, have a definite, clear, practical ideal – a goal, an objective. Second, have the necessary means to achieve your ends – wisdom, money, materials, and methods. Third, adjust your means to that end.

Thus, you need to think through what motivates you to succeed.

The traditional route to deputy headship is through the post of year head or curriculum leader – the so-called middle managers. However, being a good middle manager is not enough to take you to the next stage. The advertisements for deputy headteachers in the *Times Educational Supplement* are testament to the fact that more is required if you are to progress beyond leading a curricular or pastoral team. A typical advertisement is shown in the box overleaf. It should give you an idea of what kind of person a school looks for to be its deputy head, and of the skills and knowledge that you will have to be able to demonstrate.

Lakey Lane High School

DEPUTY HEADTEACHER
GROUP 6

Salary Range L14–L16
Roll: 950 pupils, 230 in the Sixth Form

Required for September, an outstanding well-qualified teacher with vision, energy and proven leadership ability to join a highly motivated Senior Management Team.

We are looking to appoint an excellent classroom practitioner who will

- Have a clear understanding of current educational issues
- Inspire and lead a highly professional and committed staff
- Appreciate the value of community, business and multicultural links
- Have the determination to make an impact
- Have the ability to turn strategic vision into practical reality.

Further details and application forms are available from Laura Kerry on 01234 56789. Closing date for applications 1 April.

There are a number of experiences which you need to acquire. Not all of these are essential, but a blend of them will certainly prepare you for the tasks ahead. These skills and experiences can be classified as follows:

- further study and qualifications
- whole-school issues and strategic planning

- leading cross-curricular initiatives (work with a group of teachers from other curriculum areas on particular projects)
- curriculum innovation
- creating additional value

Further study and qualifications

After a long day delivering high-quality lessons the prospect of picking up a set of academic texts and producing an essay may seem unattractive. To see further qualifications and study purely in this context is to miss the important contribution that embarking on a course can bring.

It is important that as a profession we recognise the importance of further study and there has been considerable discussion in the recent past to support this assertion. The personal and professional growth of teachers is closely related to pupil growth. One of the most significant critical interventions you can make is to invest in your own learning and seek out ways to participate in innovation and research. Brighouse and Woods (1999) describe one secondary school's research and innovation programme for one year:

- an examination of continuity and progression in English through a review of work done in Year 6
- researching attitudes to teaching and learning in Years 8 and 9 through interviews and pupil questionnaires, in partnership with a local university
- an investigation into the research skills of particular groups of pupils using the Internet and the school library
- teaching boys separately from girls in certain GCSE subjects, in order to ascertain the impact on raising achievement
- introducing and researching the effectiveness of a mentoring programme for Year 10 pupils

What is particularly noteworthy about these projects is that they all include elements of investigation and research. The information gathering is not confined to an audit; it is more than that, it is to seek out information, to reflect on practice and to measure the effectiveness of particular initiatives.

It is possible to appear self-serving when advocating the benefits of further study; however, by focusing attention on the work that teachers do and linking this work to further study, the benefit to the school of higher-level qualifications becomes clear.

A very wide range of courses is available to teachers, including diploma NVQ, MA and M.Ed courses. Supported self-directed study (as pioneered by the Open University) is one option. You may prefer the discipline of attending a local university, perhaps weekly, to hear lectures, prepare essays and the like. The advantage of this approach lies in the obligation to attend on a particular day and time. The Open University, like others which have developed 'distance learning' courses, produces materials that support self-directed study. The course books are well written and the study guides are produced in such a way as to make them accessible to a person studying alone. Added to this, the OU offers tutorials (both group and individual). Every student is allocated a course tutor and a counsellor, who are a good source of support both academically and personally. Further, some courses include summer schools where you meet other students for a period of time to consider the issues raised in greater depth. However, this kind of study requires a highly disciplined approach; you need to allocate your time to it as if you were attending lectures. The benefit of studying in a formal university setting is the frequency of contact; the benefit of supported distance learning is the flexibility of the study arrangements.

A number of courses are available, most on management subjects. The study guide for the Open University's course on educational management sets out the aims as follows:

- to promote the investigation of issues facing managers as the basis for improving practice
- to improve your ability to apply knowledge of educational management to your own place of work or one close to you, and to reflect upon your own practice and that of others
- to improve your ability to examine management issues critically and objectively and make recommendations for improved practice

- to increase your management potential and prepare you for more senior positions should you wish
- to provide direct benefit to your place of work, or your host institution, by generating concrete recommendations for improved practice based on rigorous and objective examinations of current management issues

Taking each of these in turn, it is possible to see how valuable such a course (and this is merely included as an example, rather than an endorsement) could be for you.

Firstly, you must develop an understanding of the current issues that affect the leadership and management of schools. It is difficult to explain to those joining the profession just how turbulent the past few years have been. The introduction of the National Curriculum, changes to the qualifications structure, threshold assessment, advanced skills teachers, etc. – the changes have been longed for but have constituted a serious challenge to the management of education. You will have to look carefully at the changes that have occurred in practice and others likely to occur as time goes on. All those working in schools are constantly engaged in change; there is no steady state.

The continual drive to raise standards, the perpetual debate on how things could be done better, and the imperative to add value means that all managers are in some sense 'turnaround managers'. But this requires a deep understanding of the function and purpose of the team as a whole. The demands for organisational turnaround that have characterised the last decade have generated a number of trends in schools: internationalisation and globalisation of educational theory and practice; mergers; societal changes in the competency profile of applicants for teaching; active organisational policies to address a permanently changing environment; increased governmental influence.

Secondly, by acquiring knowledge of educational management and applying this to your own practice, you can become a reflective manager. Key leadership qualities are self-awareness and understanding your own actions. Nias *et al.* (1992) found that teachers who wanted to improve their practice shared four attitudes:

1   They accepted that it was possible to improve.
2   They were ready to be self-critical.
3   They were ready to recognise better practice than their own in schools and elsewhere.
4   They were willing to learn what had to be learned to be able to do what had been done.

Thirdly, understanding others and being able to lead and manage them do not constitute an exact science reducible to cause and effect analysis. On the contrary, particular scenarios suggest different interpretations. In many ways the practice of management is about developing an understanding of how people interact and behave. The ability to examine critically the circumstances in which you work is crucial to any leader's development. Further, to be able to demonstrate an understanding rooted in theory gives an argument the potency that facilitates the growth of the organisation. The ability to put forward alternatives is important. The problems which face a senior team daily can too easily be regarded as intractable. Fresh eyes bring new solutions; new people bring new perspectives. To be a school leader you must be able to think through a problem, identify the constraints, and propose a solution. This ability is usually learned through experience and through a theoretical framework on which to base judgements. Without grounded theory, a solution can lack conviction.

There is no doubt that teachers who are hungry for career success bring a huge amount to any school. When this is combined with further study, the effect can be transformational. The purpose of professional development should not be seen as simply preparing you for the next job; in some cases the lessons learnt will not be required until much later. However, committing yourself to a programme of professional development in a suitable context will undoubtedly be beneficial to your school. It will gain from your enthusiasm and reflective practice. As an individual, you will grow with the experience.

It is important to appreciate that the benefits of further study and qualifications are not confined to the acquisition of letters after your name and enhanced career prospects. By undertaking further study while working full time (which is what most teachers have to do) you will learn to organise your time and be productive at all times.

No consideration of further study would be complete without reference to your subject. Typically, you will wish to study for a research degree in your subject (for example, in English Literature, Music, Mathematics, etc.) after completing your first degree. Such a course may provide you with more opportunities in your particular context. For example, if you are working in a strongly academic school (for example, a selective grammar or public school), then further study in your subject may be especially appreciated. To undertake this kind of study is a serious matter; research that is unrelated to your 'day job' will increase the pressure on you. But the change in gear necessitated by the study may provide you with the impetus and motivation you need to complete it. My Mathematics supervisor supported my work to the extent of giving me tutorials in the evening at his house. Certainly, attendance at the university during the day would have been difficult, as I was in my first few years of teaching.

The issue of time management is relevant at this stage. Certainly to do a professional development course after a day at work is demanding in terms of both commitment and sheer physical and mental energy. This is one reason why it is worth doing these courses early in your career. The first few years in the job are spent on lesson preparation and learning the craft of the classroom, but then you may find you are able to reflect on your practice. At this stage some form of professional development in the form of study is valuable.

It is useful to think of professional development as being a necessary and consistent part of the job. But managing it will take commitment, requiring you to dedicate blocks of time to the work. However, the closer the relationship of the study to the day job, the easier it becomes. I studied Mathematics and my thesis was on Algebra. It didn't relate directly to my work and so a significant change of mindset was required to do the research. But my MA in educational management was more closely related as I was at the time a middle manager.

Cost is an issue too. It is worth applying to your headteacher to see if resources are available to help you fund the course. However, a number of considerations must be borne in mind:

- in-service training (INSET) funds are often heavily committed and so you should discuss your plans before the school development budget is constructed (so that your funds are included).
- you need to be able to show how the school will benefit from your attendance at a course
- a school is unlikely to commit funds to you if you have declared that you intend to leave soon
- it will be easier for the school to find the money if you are able to part-fund your course
- your proposal to the headteacher should set out the benefits of your doing the course to the school and to you. You need to be able to cost your attendance at the course; for example, if the course requires attendance during the day then the cost of supply cover will need to be built in.

Whole-school issues and strategic planning

It is important to be able to demonstrate that you have the organisational ability to do the job of deputy headteacher. Equally vital, however, is facilitative skill; it is a feature utilised daily. By this I mean the ability to bring people together (in groups ranging up to the whole staff), to work as a group, and achieve an outcome. As teachers, we do this every day when working with a class. However, the skill that is required when working with a group of adults needs careful consideration.

One way to acquire such skill is to chair a working group. For example, you might lead a group looking at the behaviour policy of the school. There are a number of stages to this and by examining each you will be able to establish a methodology.

1 Identify the issue

There are a number of sources for the issues to be identified. Subject-related issues may, on further discussion with colleagues turn out to be school issues. Inspection reports may present a topic for a working group. There is no shortage of issues to be addressed in schools today.

2 Raise the issue with the school leadership team

Some caution has to be exercised at this stage. If you decide to take the issue to the leadership team (and the procedure for doing this will vary from school to school) the way in which you present it will be very important. In some schools, the leadership team will be open to suggestions and will welcome anyone who raises any matter. In others, suggestions may be seen as critical, and so much care will be needed. However, anyone who is considering a senior management role will need considerable tact and diplomacy; this is a good forum to practise them. Whatever the climate, presenting a whole-school issue in a way which establishes the need for further inquiry and proposes action be taken in the light of research and consideration shows proactive leadership.

3 Establish a contract with the leadership team

At the outset it is vital to establish a contract with the leadership team. Some organisations have quite loose structures in which various members can come together under a particular umbrella and collaborate in an informal manner. More typical, perhaps, is a structured approach where, as chair of the working group, you establish the outline plan for the work of the group, setting down what should be done and stating the purpose and reporting process. By establishing the scope of the group (to research, report and recommend), the leadership team can choose whether to direct the task or delegate it.

4 *Set up the working group*

Setting up a working group is clearly a very important task. The leadership team of the school may wish to be involved, and the discussions held with subject leaders may suggest a particular membership. The cocktail of the group membership will reflect the needs of the organisation and the importance it attaches to the remit of the group. The way to set up a group is to ask people to join it, and they are usually flattered. But it is also important to publicise the group in advance so that anyone who wants to join has the opportunity to do so. In this way you get a blend of people who are committed to the task ahead.

5 *Establish the remit of the group*

Holding a meeting is naturally the first step towards getting the group to address the issue at stake. When the matter is wide-ranging there are advantages to having an open meeting, i.e. one without an agenda. This gives the group the freedom to explore the issue in any way it wishes, but does require skilled chairmanship. Also, given the busy life of a school, people prefer to know what the focus of the group's work is going to be. Too often, an open meeting can degenerate into a 'moaning' session (particularly if the focus is behaviour) where little is achieved. However, it is important not to present yourself as the one with all the answers, prompting the question 'Why do we have a working group when you've already decided what to do?' Another method, perhaps, would be to write some kind of paper for discussion or to publish a fairly loose agenda giving the broad areas under consideration. Discussion will then become easier, as everyone will know what is at issue. One way to stimulate discussion is to ask people to work in groups and share their findings during the meeting. The outcomes of the first meeting should be as follows:

- the remit of the group is set down
- the terms of the group are established
- the time scale is known

- the reporting lines are made clear
- minutes or papers recording the outcomes and action points are produced.

6 Research the issue

There are a numbers of ways in which school issues can be researched. One of these is by a questionnaire. The advantage of such a research tool is that, within the school context, a high return can be anticipated. Unfortunately, writing a good questionnaire takes time and skill. There are useful reference books (see 'References and suggestions for further reading,' p. 26) that comment on the efficacy of different research methods. Other ways of collecting information include interviews and other surveys. Whatever means of surveying are chosen, the resulting data should inform the group on the research questions; the data therefore have to be collected in such a way that they can be interrogated through a database and deductions can be made. An important learning point for anyone embarking on such a project is to ensure that the data collection occurs when there is time to process it. Sometimes it is possible to set up the database and then negotiate the data input with the administrative support team. As the person leading the group, you should ensure that the workload is evenly spread across the group. It might seem easier to do all the work yourself, but you would then miss out on the opportunity to practise delegation skills.

7 Discuss the findings

At a subsequent meeting the group will want to discuss the findings from the research and begin to draw some conclusions. Preparing for such a meeting takes some thought; you have to ensure that the outcomes and recommendations are commensurate with the remit of the group. It is no good researching an issue, discovering completely different problems from those you started out with, and suggesting a course of action that the leadership team have not sanctioned. To do so would be at best irritating. If the outcomes of the research raise further issues, then the recommendation needs to be that 'further consideration should be given to . . .'.

8 *Produce an action plan*

The action plan is an important document, setting out the following:

- the findings of the research
- why action needs to be taken
- the proposed steps
- the implementation proposals, including time scale, INSET needs, budget considerations, etc.
- the expected outcomes of the implementation
- the requirement for monitoring, evaluation and reviewing

This should be a group effort, presented as the recommendations of the group.

9 *Produce a report*

As group leader, you must produce a report that sets out the findings of the group and makes the full range of data available. It should include features such as:

- the remit of the group
- how it was constituted
- the research brief
- the research findings
- the action plan

10 *Present the report and secure commitment to the action plan*

At this stage, the report should be presented to the leadership team for consideration. When discussing the report and action plan with the leadership team, you must ensure that they fully comprehend the implementation recommendations. By explaining the data, you will be able to show the need for action, according to the remit and functioning of the group.

11 Implement the action plan

12 Monitor the implementation through an evaluation and review process

No process is complete without some form of review. The group was established to address a need; the imperative for action was provided by the research. Implementation must follow if the recommendations were designed to address the issues. Monitoring, evaluating and reviewing the team's work strengthen the organisation's work.

Leading cross-curricular initiatives

The benefits of cross-curricular work are immense and some of the most exciting work that is done in schools comes under this heading.

A colleague, Kate, who is head of Art, described a cross-curricular project that she had organised. In the course of a conversation, she and a History teacher discovered a shared interest in a battle that had been fought near the school site. Kate's idea was to do a piece of work around this battle. This is how she went about it:

1 Decide the cross-curricular theme, that is the battle.
2 Discuss the ideas with a partner (the History teacher). The main idea was to produce an enactment of the battle: students would be in period costume and a whole range of work would be done in Art, English, History, Textiles, Mathematics and Drama to bring the project together.
3 Decide on the outcome: the children would perform their

enactment on a particular day to an invited audience and create an exhibition for people to view.

4   Hold a planning meeting at which the interested parties would produce an action plan and detailed proposals that could be taken to the Senior Management Team for approval. The plan needed to include the curriculum objectives, a rationale for the project, a budget plan, staffing and some idea of the planning process.

5   Plan the event.

6   Evaluate the event.

The result was a truly memorable occasion that brought the topic alive to the students. However, the benefits to Kate were more than simply an event that went well. In planning and organising it she learned to:

- construct a detailed plan
- communicate with a wide range of people
- deal with the pressure that a huge school event creates
- monitor the work of a wide range of people who were acting out of collegial interest

The ability to do these things is important, and leading cross-curricular initiatives gives us all the opportunity to work with a wider range of people. It also teaches us to trust other people. Collaborative work becomes all-important in the management of a large project that is not dependent on any kind of hierarchical imperative.

A major benefit of this kind of project is that it can give you something to talk about at interview. If you have had to put a good deal of time and energy into it, then your response is likely to be animated and show the kind of enthusiasm that any school would cherish.

Curriculum innovation

Finding ways to develop the curriculum represents a contribution that teachers at all levels can make to their school. Creating a new resource or writing a unit of work on study skills for PSHE: such ideas can make a difference to the educational experience. However, it is important to do this in the context of an overall strategy, perhaps including the following elements:

- establish the baseline data (i.e. the level students are working at)
- decide how you will measure progress (i.e. how you will know whether your innovation has made a difference)
- decide how you will share the process, the resources and the outcomes of your work
- decide how you will engage the support of others in the organisation to develop your work to best effect

These are challenging questions but attention to them will enable a project to be evaluated thoroughly and provide you with the means to describe your work to a wider audience.

Creating additional value

The job of a school leader is a demanding one and requires a good deal of stamina and a commitment to going the extra mile. Adding value to the organisation is one way in which you can set out what your values are and demonstrate your ability to cope with new challenges and use your own initiative.

As a school leader you need to be organised, thorough and considerate of the people with whom you work. As you try out different things you learn to take risks, not with children's education but with your own reputation. By challenging yourself constantly, by evaluating your progress and constantly reflecting on the work you do, you become a better practitioner.

The school leader's need for decision-making skills: an example

Much of the daily life of a school leader is spent making decisions, sometimes far-reaching ones such as major curriculum initiatives, more often responses to immediate problems where the decision will be very important to the people concerned but short-lived in the grand scheme. The wisdom that this requires is considerable as the decisions may carry great significance. To illustrate the ways in which these issues can be raised at this level, the example of the management of the GCSE options process is used.

Choosing GCSE subjects: some of the issues

Every year many children choose their optional subjects for GCSE. Nearly all these children are making such a choice for the first time. The previous thirteen or fourteen years have been characterised by prescription and commonality. Suddenly, they are required to make decisions that will have long-term implications for them. By making the decision to choose a science-based course, they may neglect languages; by choosing a humanities-based course, they may neglect the arts. It is rarely polarised to that extent but we have all seen children and their parents agonising over what subjects to choose. Some children have an embarrassment of choice: all their teachers want them to do 'their' subject; in sharp contrast, there are other children whom nobody wants.

On the face of it, managing the options seems a quite easy undertaking. Firstly, you ask everyone what they want to do; secondly, you collate the requirements; thirdly, you publish lists of who is going to study with whom. Simple! However, managing such a process can teach you some very valuable lessons about school leadership.

First decisions: free choice or blocks

Firstly, you have to decide whether to allow a free choice of all subjects, a restricted choice, or some kind of blocking arrangement. By presenting the process as a free choice (with or without guidance), your school makes an important statement, namely that all subjects have equal status. However, if 100 people want to do, for example, GCSE ICT and eleven want to do GCSE Textiles, then some difficult decisions have to be made. Suppose, then, that there are just two people capable of teaching ICT to GCSE level and three Textiles teachers, and the issues of staff-led curricula and possible redeployment or redundancy come to the fore. In addition, giving pupils free choice risks incurring the problem of what to do when group sizes are too big or too small and some further selection is required. If you decide to offer a restricted choice (for example, by making certain subjects compulsory, such as Double Science, Technology or ICT), you highlight the comparative worth of subjects. And what do you do when some-one doesn't want to do that compulsory subject for a good reason?

Option blocks offer a popular solution. They permit a close relationship between the staff analysis and the cohort; it is in every sense a staff-led curriculum, with all the inherent dangers that this can bring. Further, anyone who has led a discussion with staff on the content of option blocks knows well the difficulty of gaining and sustaining agreement on them.

Many of these issues involve school leadership; they are about what the headteacher wants for the school. However, the teachers who involve themselves in such a process should use this as an opportunity to consider the leadership and management issues that arise from any situation.

Second decisions: how to present and collate the information

As options co-ordinator, you may have to decide how the information is to be presented to the students and their parents. You have a number of possible choices.

A BOOKLET

The advantage of a booklet is that all the necessary information can be presented in a common format and the process set down as a point of reference. However, when committing policy to paper, your school needs to be sure that the message it is sending is congruent with its aims; words reveal much about the values an organisation has for its clients.

There may be a parents' evening, an options evening, mini-interviews or a blend of these. The advantage of this method is that it encourages joint decision-making. However, you will have to make sure that all the information and all the messages are delivered in a consistent manner. Teachers have sometimes subverted the free choice offered to students by denigrating subjects other than their own. Such behaviour is inexcusable, but it does happen. You will also have to make sure that the messages reach all the people concerned: if you have ever organised a parents' evening you will appreciate the challenge of a 100 per cent attendance rate.

Once the process has been established, how is the information passed on to you, as the options co-ordinator? Most schools have the SIMS system, and the options package provides the co-ordinator with an efficient means of collating all the information and being able to present it to school leaders. This brings us to the matter of communication. How do you communicate with heads of subjects anxious to know who is going to choose their subject, heads of year who may have parents contacting them and, of course, students who want to know about their curriculum over the next two years?

Making difficult decisions

Table 1.1 sets out the number of students applying to do certain subjects. The number of classes you will be able to support is six (i.e. 150/6 = 25, average class size).

Presented with this information, as options co-ordinator, you will have to make some difficult choices. Table 1.1 is not designed to tease out all the possible decisions and scenarios that could be considered:

Table 1.1 Students' selection of their options

Subject	Number selecting	Max/min numbers
History	34	32
Business studies	39	32
Resistant materials	22	25
Graphics	18	20
Textiles	14	25
Food	15	25
Child development	8	25

the data are too sparse to accomplish this usefully. One way forward would be to see all those who have chosen Child development and talk to them about making an alternative choice. So you see each child and explain the situation; some will agree readily and others will be more reluctant. They all take a letter home to their parents explaining what you have discussed and the change their child has agreed to make. The next morning (or even days later), you receive a long letter from a parent saying how upset her daughter is, how giving up Child development will make her career impossible – a catalogue of concerns about how the change will affect the child. As the options co-ordinator you thought you had done everything necessary, having discussed it carefully with the child. A simple, straightforward task, undertaken in a calm, caring and considerate manner, has resulted in a very upset child and distressed parents. This example is given to illustrate the human dimension of school management. It also shows that small decisions can cause great upset to the people involved. In your drive to achieve efficiency, never forget that the children in your school have parents who love them and want the best for them. When learning to manage a school, and practising the craft of leadership and management, always remember that the people with whom we deal have feelings and needs. The small world of a child can be devastated by a teacher's decision. Thus, a benefit of learning new jobs in a context of further study is indeed that you learn to reflect upon your own practice and that of others.

Building up a portfolio of experiences

The process described above is an example of how your work in one of the regular features of the school calendar can provide an opportunity for some high-level thinking and action. The benefits of such involvement are that:

- it gives you experience of leading a whole-school project
- the project is relatively short term, covering a period of about two months
- you gain experience of dealing with children you might not otherwise know (and frequently as deputy you will have to deal with children you don't know)
- you will have to deal with a large amount of information
- you will develop your ability to work with a wide staff group
- you will have to consider how to balance the economic choices with the demands of children

One of the major benefits of this type of work is the opportunity to reflect on your practice. This is very important. A teacher should undertake these development tasks for two reasons: to acquire skills, and to acquire experience. Carrying out such a task may make you decide never to do it that way again (or even never to do it again!). It is very important for you to analyse why something worked, which parts didn't work well and what impact your efforts had on the process itself. If your impact was negligible, perhaps you hadn't thought creatively about the process, or perhaps your handling of the task was so skilful that it appeared effortless and exact. But the ability to analyse a procedure and extract learning points from the outcomes is an essential skill.

Summing up

The purpose of this chapter was to explain why as a career teacher you need to be proactive about acquiring skills and experiences. The first step is to be an excellent teacher and the OfSTED criteria are a good source of guidance. The modern career teacher is a self-aware leader and reflective manager. The ability to reflect is grounded in an understanding of organisational issues and theory. By using theory as a reference point, you learn to reflect critically on your actions and those of the people around you. It is important to tackle a range of school issues and the paradigm for leading a working group provides a structure to the task ahead.

Action points

- Set out to be an excellent teacher.
- Study the OfSTED criteria and use them to enhance your work.
- Consider why you want to be a deputy headteacher.
- Understand the benefits of further study, and make plans to complete appropriate courses.
- Appreciate that the acquisition of skills and experience takes time. It is also very personal. The skills required of a school leader are considerable. They require maturity of thought and clarity of vision.
- By establishing a process where you can lead a group and facilitate its work, you practise important skills.
- Leading a working group enables you to consider the management models and your own practice.
- Leadership is not just about being the 'chair'. It can involve curriculum innovation at any level.
- An essential skill is to be able to plan, to assess progress and to evaluate a project. Use baseline data as a starting point.
- Develop a reputation for risk taking. Your confidence and your skill will grow as you try things out and evaluate their success. Reflecting on your personal practice is essential if you are to lead others.

References and suggestions for further reading

Born M. and Jansen P. (1997) 'Selection and Assessment During Organisational Turnaround' in Herriot P. and Anderson N. (eds) *International Handbook of Selection and Assessment* John Wiley, Chichester

Brighouse T. and Woods D. (1999) *How to Improve Your School* Routledge, London

Handy C. (1981) *Understanding Organizations* Penguin, London

Handy C. (1995) *The Age of Unreason* Arrow, London

Nias J., Southworth G. and Campbell P. (1992) *Whole School Curriculum Development in the Primary School* Falmer, London

Open University 1995 *E828: Educational Management in Action Study Guide* prepared by Bennett N. *et al.* The Open University, Milton Keynes

Open University (1991) *E621 Methodology Handbook* (1991) prepared by Faulkner D., Swann J., Baker S., Bird M. and Carty J., Open University, Milton Keynes

2 Dear Headteacher, Thank you for inviting me for interview

Monday, 15 October

Things to do today:

1   Now that I've received further information from the school about the deputy head job, I need to plan for the interview next week.
2   See the head and ask for permission to attend the interview – confirm details.
3   Start thinking about the kind of questions they will ask and how the presentation will be organised.
4   Decide what to wear.
5   Plan teaching of my classes so that they can be 'left' next week.

One of the things that has struck me over the past few weeks is that the interview is only one part of the recruitment process.

I read the person specification and the job description last evening. These two documents are very important. When I wrote the application I made sure that I addressed every point. In some ways this was easy to do because my skills fit exactly what they are looking for. Looking through the essential/desirable list, I have all the characteristics in both columns – so that is good.

Thinking about what to wear. I've always gone to interviews wearing my standard school clothes – never done the 'interview suit' business – and it works for me. I think it's important to be comfortable and so wearing anything new or that I'm not used to could be a mistake. I think that the school has to be happy with 'me'. It's easy to want to try to be the person I think they want just because I want the job.

At the last interview I attended I think that's why it went wrong – it was for a pastoral deputy. I thought that they were looking for a certain type of person and I think I tried to convey the impression that I was that person. I didn't get the job and I think in hindsight that this was a good thing. It wouldn't have worked there. I think that I would have found the work frustrating and boring. My strength is in the curriculum. I have my views on the ways in which assessment can be carried out to maximum effect. I have opinions on how the quality of teaching can be improved and I'm good at systems. I think that the model of pastoral/curriculum deputy has been subjected to quite a lot of discussion but I do tend to lean the curriculum way.

The headteacher phoned to invite me to the interview. I think that this is a nice touch. I think that the advice I was given by my current head – 'be aware that you are on interview from the moment you drive on to the car park' – is good.

In this chapter we look more closely at the application and interview process. Of course this starts with seeing the advertisement. The one illustrated in Chapter 1 is shown again here (Figure 2.1). It is important to read it with care and to consider what the job is all about. The application – whether by CV, letter or form – is obviously the first stage in the process and so it is vital that your skills and experiences are shown to match the requirements specified.

If, when you read through the advertisement, you can think of things about yourself that relate to the points listed, then this is a good start. If the job sounds completely alien to you, then it is unlikely to be the right one for you.

When you ask a school for 'further details' about the job, then typically you receive a range of information, including:

- a letter from the headteacher
- information about the job (salary level, title of the post, etc.)
- job description
- person specification
- prospectus
- application form and request for a letter of application

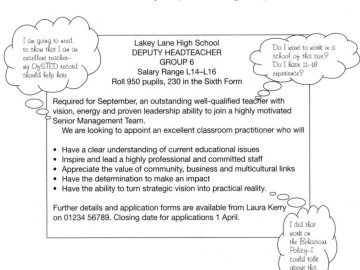

Figure 2.1 Matching skills to requirements

It is clearly important to read all this information through very carefully to assess whether the school is a place where you would want to work and, moreover, whether your skill set fits the profile that is being sought. This chapter examines a number of elements of the application process.

The job description

The job description will set out the tasks and the responsibilities of the post, as in the following example.

Job title: Deputy Headteacher

Salary: L14–L16

Responsible to: Headteacher

Main purpose of the job: promoting and supporting the vision and professional leadership of the school, ensuring high-quality education for all its pupils and improving standards of achievement; promoting and implementing governors' policies to achieve school aims; creating an environment and managing specific resources to promote and secure the achievement of both pupils and staff; deputising for the headteacher in his absence and carrying out statutory duties as stated in the current School Teachers Pay and Conditions Document; working towards the National Professional Qualification for Headteachers (NPQH).

Teaching and learning: providing a model of excellent classroom practice; classroom observation and development of strategies to show good practice; monitoring and enhancing the quality of teaching and learning; reviewing and developing the curriculum with the Senior Management Team.

Leading and managing: staff welfare; induction of new staff; chairing pastoral development group; developing and monitoring pastoral policies; co-ordinating and overseeing the work of heads of year, including option choices, PSHE, tutorial programme, attendance and assemblies; dealing with emergencies and with discipline.

Efficient and effective use of staff and resources: planning, managing and monitoring the pastoral system and staff development within the agreed budget; oversight of premises issues; lunchtime supervision.

The point of a job description (however vague) is that it sets out what the deputy headteacher will have to do. It often is vague because being part of the school leadership team means that you have to be prepared to do 'anything' and 'everything'. Further, the relationship between the headteacher and deputies is at its best when everyone knows what they have to do but are prepared to 'muck in' when circumstances require.

Person specification

The person specification for the job of deputy headteacher can be considered in sections. The first section is usually about qualifications. You will have to give your professional qualification and your degree. At this level a good honours degree is essential. Evidence of further study and/or qualifications is often required, the reason being that the task of school leadership is so complex that an MA degree (or the like) may be needed as evidence of intellectual and professional competence. Moreover, the inclusion of the NPQH (or part-qualification) is growing in popularity. You may be asked for proof of your qualifications, an effect of the few cases where claims have been found to be fraudulent.

The second requirement is for a certain level of experience. This can vary, but will normally be related to the type of school you have worked in (for example, you may need experience 'of more than your comprehensive school', or to have shown a 'commitment to selective education'). Some people secure promotions having only worked in one school but these are rare. Moving to a new school at the appropriate stage of your career will enable you to build up a body of experience. It can be difficult enough to see your way forward through a complex set of organisational requirements. If you are blinkered by lack of experience, a difficult job will be much harder. A further stipulation is experience of working at a senior level, perhaps as head of a curriculum area or head of year. It will be interesting to note the effect of the Leadership Team. Or to become deputy headteacher you may be asked to show experience of 'working in the leadership team'. A critical element of this section is experience of leading a successful team and often of managing change.

Personal attributes are the third requirement. Phrases used to describe the necessary characteristics include:

- the ability to work well as a team member
- excellent interpersonal skills
- the ability to communicate effectively with a variety of audiences

- the ability to work well under pressure
- energy, vigour and perseverance

These characteristics are not unusual. They reflect the fact that leading a school is not just about being able to do certain jobs. It is about leading groups of people and working in a variety of different ways.

Skills and competences are the fourth requirement. You will need to show that you have:

- significant IT skills (often knowledge of the SIMS system)
- the ability to lead, motivate and support a team, delegating where necessary
- excellent classroom skills
- evidence of interest in curriculum development

This list is not exhaustive but is intended to demonstrate the range of skills and competences that may be required.

The point of the person specification is to set out what sort of person is required. As such, it identifies those key features that must be addressed in the letter of application. Put simply, the application process is designed around the person specification.

Putting these together

The job description and person specification should together form the basis for your entire application process. This has a number of phases:

- writing the letter of application and completing the application form
- being invited for and preparing for the interview process
- the interview process, including panel interviews, tours of the school, meetings with staff, presentations, group exercises, final interviews

Sometimes the applications process varies considerably. It's very important to ensure that you do everything it says to do and nothing more. It's very irritating when going through lots of applications to find piles of CVs if they are not required. Similarly, if you are asked for a two-sided letter, then a four-page one is likely to be rejected straight away.

Curriculum vitae

Some applications will require a curriculum vitae. It is a good thing to keep yours updated, with details of courses etc. that you have attended. There are packages that will produce these for you.

The important thing to realise is that there is no standard way of producing a CV. However, it should contain the following sections:

- **personal details**: name, address, telephone numbers, email address, etc.
- **career history** (in chronological order): it is useful, especially when applying to a different area, to give a few brief details of the schools you have worked at, for example the type of school (boys, girls, co-ed, comprehensive, grammar, etc.), number of roll, title of your post and scale. If you can summarise your job in a couple of sentences then this should be enough to show what you have done
- **qualifications**: by date, subject and grade
- **courses and professional training**: list the course, the awarding authority, duration, subjects covered
- **your current role**: a brief job description, scale or salary point and any other responsibilities (i.e. form tutor, representative on the PTA, teacher governor, etc.)
- **referees**: list by name, title, address, telephone, email and/or fax

It is worth spending time creating this document and storing it on your PC. Then, as your role develops, you can quickly add things on.

Application form and request for a letter of application

It is common to be asked for both. The application form is usually a standard one where you record personal details such as your name, address, date of birth, academic qualifications and a chronology of experience. It is important to complete it accurately. It is the first stage in the process. There are some important things to remember about filling in the form:

1   Read the letter from the headteacher that sets out what information is required. Some schools use the form for salary purposes only and so will specifically state 'Please do not enter supporting information in the space on the application form'. If this is ignored and you write in information, at best it will be ignored, at worst your whole application will be rejected because you failed to follow instructions.
2   Read through the form and use black ink or a word processor. It can be difficult to word-process on a pre-printed form. Bear in mind that the application will be photocopied a number of times for the shortlisting committees and interview panels. Therefore clear, legible handwriting is essential.
3   Check the spelling and punctuation.
4   Check to ensure that you have completed all the required sections of the form – this may include monitoring sections. The information shown in the box opposite is always required somewhere in an application: if you haven't written it anywhere, check the form.

Writing a letter of application is more difficult and requires a considerable amount of time. The most important thing to do is to link your skills and experiences to the person specification. Each of the criteria will be assessed at some point during the application process and you need to show how your competences match those required. Table 2.1 sets out how different tasks can be linked to the criteria.

Name

Address

Telephone number

Age/date of birth

Qualifications

Current school and post

Chronology of experience

Referees

DfEE and NI numbers

Police check

When you could start

Signature

It is difficult to prescribe exactly what you should say. So much depends on the precise requirements of the job and the specifics of your experience. However, this is beneficial: writing a letter to a particular formula would not show you to your greatest advantage. Writing a personal letter showing that the needs of the school match your skills and experience should take you on to the next stage.

1 Read through the application literature again to ensure that all the requirements have been met.
2 Try to put yourself in the mind of the headteacher, who might easily receive between fifty and two hundred applications for the deputy headship. By writing a short concise letter (two sides of A4 in a readable font) that says who you are, what you have done and how this matches the school's needs, you go a long way to demonstrating that empathy. By showing that the application is to that particular school (not a 'standard'

Table 2.1 Linking the person specification to skills and experiences

Criterion	Example
Further professional study/ qualifications	This can be shown via the application form but, it is important to show what effect the further study has had on your practice and how it brought about improvements to your school
Leading a successful team	Compare the results in public examinations across your school or before your leadership (in the case of a subject leader); the actual data are useful here
Contributing to the wider life of the school	Describe how you have been involved, emphasising your leadership skills and the responsibilities you have taken on
Good classroom practitioner	Refer to the OfSTED assessment of your teaching
Significant IT skills	Refer to your IT capability and how you have used it to improve the efficiency of the school or the effectiveness of a curriculum initiative

letter), with reference to its pertinent features, you make yourself sound interesting and worth considering.
3   Post the application in an A4 envelope with sufficient postage, in good time. Your application looks better if it is not folded in half. Do not use the school post. Many headteachers see this as dishonest and will reject such an application straight away.

References and being invited for interview

It is presumed that you know the etiquette whereby you inform your headteacher that you have made an application for a job. This is important not only for reasons of courtesy but also because your headteacher will be one of your referees. Headteachers in the same

But what about preparing an application when you already work at the school? I think that this is something that is hard to do. It is important that you take the same approach to the letter of application – but bear in mind that the school knows you. The school doesn't need to know your career history but does need to know how the skills that you have acquired over the past years will fit you for the role. The head will also want some indication that you will be able to move from your current role into the new one. The job of senior manager is different from that of subject leader and you need to show that you have the vision to look beyond your own immediate experience.

The question of references still holds, though. The headteacher can still be asked to provide a reference but it is useful to have a referee from outside the school (for example, the LEA subject adviser).

area often discuss applications informally at their meetings. Such a practice may be disagreeable and contravene official policies, but it does happen. A headteacher who learns from a fellow head-teacher that one of his or her staff is applying for another job will be embarrassed and this will place you in a bad light. More positively, your headteacher may be willing to read your application and comment upon it. This could be a useful source of valuable advice.

The process of longlisting and shortlisting takes place at the school to which the application is being made; some headteachers write for references on those who are longlisted, others only for those on the shortlist. It is becoming more common for head-teachers to send for references only after inviting people for interview. This represents a change in the traditional practice where references were sought before any invitation was offered.

In business and commerce, it is usual to make a job offer and then seek references. The change in practice does not, perhaps, represent a movement towards the business model; more likely, it reflects a growing confidence in the assessment techniques that many schools are using for the selection of their senior staff. To put it simply, schools are finding ways to assess the suitability of applicants other than the traditional reference.

One of the most important factors in the application process is your relationship with your headteacher. The role of school leader is so pivotal to the organisation's success that 'getting on' is vital. This is what can make the process of securing the post of deputy headteacher so frustrating; it is often decided on the basis of how an applicant will 'fit in' with the team. Headteachers consequently spend a lot of time ensuring that they make the right appointment. Many start to cultivate this relationship by telephoning those applicants they are inviting for interview and explaining the interview process.

This can be a very exciting moment. However, it is worth making sure that you ascertain the following details:

- the date of the interviews and the time you are required to attend
- whether you are automatically required on both days (the process usually lasts two days but there is often a 'cut' at some stage)
- how many applicants are being invited
- whether there is a presentation and, if so, on what topic and whether you will be able to use an overhead projector, ordinary projector or flipchart
- whether the details will be confirmed by post

The headteacher will usually follow up this invitation with a letter explaining the process and it is appropriate to send a reply.

There are a number of elements to the selection process. They vary in their detail, but there is sufficient generality to make the following remarks appropriate.

Arriving at the school

This is an obvious point, but it is important to know where the school is and how long it will take to get there. If necessary, telephone the school for a map. It is often worth while being early enough to see the children arrive, particularly if the school is in an area with which you are unfamiliar.

One of the most important things to remember is that everything you do and say will be noticed while you are at the school. There will be someone observing your every action; some schools, when making such an appointment, prepare a pro forma so that everyone who comes into contact with any of the candidates in any circumstances can comment. The job of deputy headteacher is always very high profile and it is vital for a school to make the right appointment.

Readers of this book will have been to interviews before, and a comment on dress may seem unnecessary. It is important to be comfortable in your clothes; wearing the 'interview suit' or specially purchased shoes may not put you at your ease. Good advice is to dress as if you were going to work on a normal day. As deputy headteacher, you are expected to be a role model for the staff in everything you do. The interview day will show whether you are capable of that role. It is also very important that your dress reflects the person you are. When appointing a deputy headteacher, a school will appoint someone who can do the job and be 'right' for the school. Trying to be someone you are not is never a good idea. The rest of the day will be filled with the following range of activities.

Meeting with the headteacher

This will normally be the first time you have met. The purpose of such a meeting (which is usually very short) is to establish a relationship. It is an opportunity for both parties to see whether you will get along. Typical topics at this stage will include:

- polite questions, such as whether you had a good journey

- a description of something you have done recently at school
- your response to an article in the *TES* or a particular issue in the educational press

You may also be given the opportunity to ask questions. It is important to make a positive impression at this stage: one way to achieve this is to ensure that your answers are brief and considered. The opportunity for more extended dialogue will arise later. This short interview is a time for brevity.

Tour of the school

It is common for students to be used to take candidates round the school. They are usually handpicked and will be asked what they think of you afterwards. As you go round the school it is important to observe the niceties with both staff and students:

- talk to the students who are showing you round: ask them what they think about the school, what they would change, etc.
- greet the teachers into whose classes you are taken, bearing in mind, however, that they are teaching their classes and may not be able to speak to you; indeed, you should avoid too protracted a conversation as this may cause difficulties later on
- talk to the students in the classes, if appropriate; ask them about their work

This is your first opportunity to see the school at work. Formal interviews will often begin with candidates being asked to comment on the school: what is the best thing about it? What are your observations? It is important to have a positive statement to make about the working day at the school, but there is a place for making some adverse remark. If, for example, you witnessed any poor behaviour, you should make some suitable remark on it. A deputy headteacher has to notice these things.

Panel interviews

It is usual for applicants to be interviewed by small groups. These panel interviews will be composed of heads of departments, heads of year, parent governors, staff governors and, in some schools, a student representative. The topics of these interviews will normally cover:

- views on setting/mixed-ability teaching
- views on ICT
- ways of monitoring the quality of teaching
- support for staff
- your way of dealing with particular situations

The objective of these panel interviews is often to give the staff the opportunity to have their say. It is therefore necessary to demonstrate to the panel that you are a sound practitioner, someone who understands the job of teaching. Subject leaders will be looking for someone who will support their work on the curriculum – who knows about teaching, knows the issues affecting their subject, and is aware of the person-management issues they face. Year heads will be looking for someone who has ideas on pupil management, who will support their work, and understands the stresses of dealing with difficult students and parents. Parent governors are looking for someone who will, among other things, ensure that their children receive a quality education and are happy.

Group exercises

Group exercises are becoming an increasingly important part of the assessment process. The purpose is to see how well you function in a team situation. The job of deputy headteacher involves facilitating groups and working as part of a team. Group exercises are, therefore, an appropriate activity. The exercise can vary. In some cases, a group of four candidates will discuss an issue. In others you may be required to chair part of a discussion on some management scenario. Typical scenarios and topics for discussion include:

- raising attainment for a particular year group
- tackling a behaviour issue
- responding to a parental complaint
- preparing a press statement
- responding to a personnel issue

The working of the group will probably be observed. The objective is to see how you respond to others: are you a leader? Do you listen to others? Are you too dominant or too submissive? It is important to maintain some perspective on this type of activity. The best advice is to act naturally, as if you were doing the job. Trying to 'second guess' what type of person is being sought can only lead to error.

In-tray exercises

A typical scenario is to be given a paper tray that simulates the in-tray of the deputy headteacher. It will usually contain a range of circulars, letters, memos and the like. You should be able to identify which are important and be able to justify your choice. In most cases, a letter from a parent is the most important item; circulars can be read at home. The objective is to see whether you can prioritise your work and how you respond to the many pieces of paper that will come your way when in post. Expect to discuss your response to a letter in the in-tray in the formal interview.

Psychometric tests

The use of psychometric tests is increasing – although they are expensive. These tests are discussed in detail in Chapter 4. Any school wishing to use psychometric tests will need to employ someone from outside to administer them and interpret the results. The objective is to see what kind of person you are and how you will fit in with the rest of the team.

The cut

Many schools eliminate some candidates before the final interview. Some take all candidates through the whole process, but this is relatively unusual because of the time needed to interview people properly. Normally, two or three people go through to the last stage.

It is not at all nice to be rejected. However, feedback is essential if you are to learn from the experience. It is a professional courtesy to be offered feedback and it is advisable to accept this offer. If you feel particularly upset, it may be worth waiting for a day or so before you take up the offer, by which time you should be better able to receive any advice and counsel.

The final interview

The Chair of Governors will preside at the final interview. The panel will include some of the people who have interviewed you already, and there may be other governors too. This is the big interview, where the decision on the appointment is made. All the issues which have arisen from the previous activities will be explored here. The panel will want to know why they should appoint you and whether you can convince them that you are right for their school.

You can expect such an interview to last about an hour and be very searching. The governing body will be making its second most important appointment (the first being the headteacher). It will be deciding how to spend a considerable portion of the staffing budget. Members will want to be sure of you and you will need to be sure of them. The nature of the questions will vary but the following list gives likely topics:

- What you think about the school?
- What is your leadership model?
- What is your management model?
- How would you cope with a difficult situation?
- What did you learn about yourself when tackling the difficult situation?

- What are your development needs?
- What are your strengths and weaknesses?
- What advice would you give in a particular situation?
- How do you see your relationship with the staff?
- How do you see your relationship with the headteacher?
- What is your view of the curriculum?
- What is your response to national educational issues?
- Do you want to be a headteacher?

This list is not exhaustive, but it illustrates the diversity of the topics that you may need to discuss. It is therefore important for you to consider all these issues before any interview; you are applying to be a senior member of staff and as such will need to have an opinion that stands up to the rigours of interrogation.

One of the words most often used in advertisements and letters is 'vision'. Schools want to appoint people with 'vision' – they want 'visionary' people. But what does this mean within the context of education at the start of a new century? The next section explores these ideas. It is important to think through these issues for yourself. The job of deputy headteacher is not restricted to the functional aspects of timetabling, cover, dealing with children's problems and the like. In a very real sense, the job of deputy head involves being able to think through issues and to look ahead to the future. This is particularly the case where the deputy sees this role as preparation for headship.

A vision for the future: thinking the unthinkable

Handy (1995) begins his discussion of change with the assertion that continuous change is comfortable change. The past is then the guide to the future. One way in which British society differs from American society is that explanations and rationales in Britain are rooted in history and tradition whereas in America, explanations are functional. However, even in Britain the status quo may no longer point to the best way forward. In that sense, Handy asserts, we are entering an 'Age of Unreason', when the future, in so many areas, is there to be shaped by us and for us; this is a time when the only prediction that will hold true is that no predictions will hold true. This is scary stuff. However, its purpose is to emphasise to all those who aspire to lead our schools that different ways of thinking are necessary. Further, the person who has the vision for the future is the one who will shape thinking and determine the course.

Recent changes in the school environment and the balance of managerial responsibilities have highlighted the importance of staff recruitment and selection. The changing nature of education has resulted in increased pressure on schools to become more enterprising and flexible in response to the needs of the entire client base. The use of the term 'client' is a deliberate one.

Legislation relating to schools, colleges and institutions of higher education has stimulated two movements that have great significance for the nature of management in education. Firstly, the relative autonomy of institutions has been enhanced. Schools have greater control over their own affairs and more scope for self-government and 'local' management. Secondly, the opportunity for users of educational services such as parents, students and employers to choose between institutions (and in some cases, to exercise influence within them) has been extended. This has created a climate of heightened interinstitutional competition and a sense of greater dependence on external audiences. Both developments imply a more explicit, visible and broad-ranging managerial role for many staff in education and a need for them to acquire new skills and competences to enable them to carry it out effectively.

A further issue is the relationship with the governing body. How do you see this? This can be difficult when your experience of them may be slight. However, the debate over foundation status, community schools and specialist status has brought this to the fore. The imperative for this debate is likely to increase as the range of specialisms increases. For many, the relationship between the school and the community it serves is critical here.

Stakeholders, clients and the environment

The concept of an institution's 'environment' is somewhat arbitrary because to suggest a definition presumes a distinction which can be erroneous and potentially misleading. It is particularly difficult to determine whether certain groups of 'stakeholders' such as pupils/ students, parents and governors should be regarded as internal or external to the institution. Where do the boundaries fall, and how permeable are they? Governors are an obvious case in point, especially given the legislation that gives them a wide-ranging set of decision-making responsibilities in major areas of a school's activities. On this basis, governors might well be 'placed' within rather than outside the institution, especially if an analogy with the board of directors is considered viable. An important part of the justification for reform of the composition of the governors was to give the 'consumer' a greater and more direct influence in institutional decision-making. Hence the substantial increase in parental and community representation on school governing bodies.

Pupils and students offer another example of this dilemma of allocation. At least for analytical purposes, from a management perspective they would generally be regarded as members of the institution. Yet they reflect the local environment in ways that are often of crucial importance for both institutional management and teaching.

The challenge facing you as an aspiring deputy headteacher is to think your way through this issue and many others. There is a challenge to the prevailing orthodoxies in the world of education. The parameters of this challenge are articulated by Bowring-Carr and West-Burnham (1997) as:

- knowledge grows out of curiosity and involvement of the individual and out of the educative relationship of the teacher and learner
- learning how to learn is the most important outcome of education
- learning is individual, subjective, contingent and communal

- the existing mind map of the learner is the starting point for all true education
- teaching is only one of the factors which influence learning
- only a small proportion of learning can take place in schools

The purpose of setting out these parameters is to emphasise that management and leadership in education have changed considerably over recent years. It is a creative and dynamic process, and when applying to be a deputy head you must articulate what education as a process means for you as a prospective school leader.

But education is not just something that happens during the five hours of daily instruction! It is no longer about telling people things — as our understanding of knowledge has changed the traditional views are challenged. As more is demanded of teachers and school leaders the imperative to work in different ways is strong — but what does this mean for a school leader?

Typically, individuals are recruited and selected to work as part of a group because they appear to have the technical skills and experiences deemed necessary for the job. This, of course, is entirely reasonable. There are a number of management models that have attempted to describe the way in which schools run. Weber (1947), the first major writer on organisational theory, defined the essentials of bureaucracy and had a significant influence on the subsequent development of this line of theory. Weber advocated a clear-cut division of labour, a hierarchical authority structure and a system of rules and regulations. In the context of a school, each manager in authority (and this applies equally to the headteacher, deputy, assistant heads and heads of departments) occupies an 'office'. In the action associated with their status, according to the commands that are issued to others, managers are subject to the impersonal order to which these actions are oriented. People who obey authority do so only in their capacity as a 'member' of the corporate group and what they obey is only 'the law'. Further, the organisation of offices follows the principle of hierarchy; that is, each lower office is under the control and supervision of a higher one. Weber argues that the purest type of exercise of legal authority is that which employs a bureaucratic administrative staff; there are several features that relate this to schools:

1   Candidates are selected on the basis of technical qualifications. They are appointed.
2   The salary scale is primarily graded according to rank in the hierarchy; but in addition to this criterion, the responsibility of the position and the requirements of the incumbent's social status may be taken into account.
3   Teaching constitutes a career. There is a system of promotion according to seniority or achievement or both. Promotion is dependent on the judgement of superiors.

The Weberian model therefore projects an image of certain 'leaders' deliberately controlling the system, but it fails to recognise the effects of the presence of personnel with 'professional' tendencies and orientations on the process of leadership and decision making in education. In a school, the overwhelming majority of staff are professionally qualified. A claim – inherent in professionalism – to self-determination in the exercise of professional functions is made in schools, not only within the remit of strictly professional competence but also in the sphere of general organisational planning and its detailed execution. Put simply, teachers at whatever level consider themselves competent to carry out their job and consider that they should have a say in both the policy and practice of school management and leadership. It is in this context that the collegial model emerged. Noble and Pym (1970) describe the 'receding locus of power' that defines such a model. The 'real' decisions always seem to be taken somewhere else. The lower-level officials or committees argue that they, of course, can only make recommendations. Departments must seek the approval of interdepartmental committees, and these in turn can only submit reports and recommendations to the general management committee. Thus decision making is not just a technical matter, a matter of considering expert advice, weighing alternatives, calculating costs and benefits and striking a balance, but of finding room to pursue a project hemmed in by decisions already taken elsewhere, not always with adequate consideration, or by other decisions yet to be taken.

However, schools have had to move on from the principle of bureaucracy and indeed collegiality to embrace other models that describe their world. The use of teams in organisational settings is increasing in the West partly because managers see teams as a medium for empowering individuals, but also because research suggests that setting group goals increases productivity (Sundstrom *et al.* 1990) and promotes innovation. While this particular research was concentrated in an industrial setting, part of it may be applicable elsewhere. The immediate practical reason for working in groups is the need to combine efforts, knowledge and skills, since many complicated tasks cannot be accomplished by one person. As organisations have grown in size and become more complicated in their structure, the need for people to work together in co-ordinated ways to achieve objectives which contribute to the overall aims of their organisation has also become clear. Co-ordinating the activities of groups with clearly defined and organisationally relevant objectives makes it easier to translate organisational strategy into practical action. How to select people for team-based work forms the subject of Chapter 4.

The pastoral deputy or the curriculum deputy

The job of deputy headteacher is becoming less polarised in terms of the curriculum/pastoral divide – and this is a good thing. Too often there has been a division that at a structural level looks attractive, but at a functional level misses the point. Marland (1985) discusses the pastoral needs of schools in relation, first of all, to the child. For Marland the child has a number of roles in school:

- the child as daughter or son: this is where the indicators of 'home' are the same crude ones of socio-economic class

- the child as pupil: in this context one of the central pastoral tasks is to help pupils learn to be pupils, for to be a pupil means to have expectations about what schools can offer and an optimism that he or she can draw on those offers
- the pupil as student: much of the school day is spent in class-rooms and is ostensibly devoted to 'school work'; but there is little to draw on when trying to analyse what 'work' means to students
- the student as 'information user'

The term 'pastoral curriculum' has often been used to cover such areas as tutorial work and personal, educational and vocational guidance. It is devised to teach the underlying facts, concepts, attitudes and skills required by the individual for personal and social development. It includes careers information, sex education and health education. The common fallacies of pastoral care include an overemphasis on individual work, an underemphasis on content, and a belief that there is no theory; rather, success depends on experience and getting to know the pupil. The fact that the pastoral curriculum has been dissociated from the examined curriculum has weakened it. Put a deputy head in charge of something under this heading and his or her role is weakened.

When pastoral care was a euphemism for 'discipline', the role of the deputy head (pastoral) was fairly straightforward: to take on intransigent cases. The role broadened to include line management of heads of year and typically included a range of tasks:

- general oversight of house/year system
- particular responsibility for the upper/lower school, boys'/girls' welfare/discipline
- liaisons with outside agencies, e.g. social services, the educational welfare officer, probation service
- attendance and admission
- school meal supervision
- aspects of daily administration, e.g. staff cover, supply staff, wet weather arrangements, duties
- school transport

- furniture and equipment
- staff welfare/development
- communications within the school, e.g. the notice board, staff discipline

It is not difficult to envisage a pastoral deputy, anxious to promote the central importance of the pastoral function, placing subtle emphases on particular aspects of the job in order to fulfil specific goals. If the school is equally anxious to accord status to its pastoral as to its academic function, it will make appropriate noises about the indivisibility of the two areas. Unfortunately, in seeking to establish a pastoral system which provided a stable and caring environment, it may have accorded undue rank and consultative status to its senior pastoral staff, and have thereby created an imbalance between its academic and pastoral functions.

The reason for this is self-evident. However elevated the philosophy informing the school's system, one of its chief functions will almost certainly be disciplinary – the maintenance of order. There is an immediacy about disorder which demands attention; something, it is felt, must be done urgently to prevent another outbreak of smoking and the pastoral system is at hand to do it. And, while the pastoral system performs acts of heroism, the academic leadership plods solid paths through the curriculum.

The curriculum deputy, in contrast, has meant the analyst and timetabler: the facilitator of the school curriculum philosophy and the person responsible for more complex administration. In that sense, therefore, the deputy's role is entirely in the gift of the headteacher, and the functions are by definition more closely circumscribed and yet more arbitrary than those of the subordinates. Everything here depends upon the relationship between the head and the deputy. However, the curriculum, though indisputably central to the school's purposes, does not exist in isolation from the rest of the institution, nor does it in practice govern it. There has to be an interaction between the multiple interests and functions of the school which are reflected in the interaction between those senior staff who share the responsibility for its effective management. Certainly an academic or curriculum deputy whose functions are entirely restricted to the activities outlined above would not be seen to make any consistent impact on the life of the school. Because once the concept of curriculum leadership is considered, it must mean moving from a passive function of placing symbols on a timetable to enquiring what those symbols actually represent. When the person with curriculum responsibility starts to ask questions of team leaders – what are your department's philosophy and practice and how do these translate into everyday life? – then he or she starts to exercise a profound and fundamental influence on school life.

The pastoral/curriculum divide still exists in many schools and there are some who will be attracted to one or other of those roles. However, in many cases it is accepted that as learning is something which permeates the entirety of school life, there cannot be a divide between what people are taught and how they are taught. It must be acknowledged that any division is structural and can be both an opportunity and a constraint.

Bowring-Carr and Burnham-West (1997) describe a world that believed in linear causality, whereas we know now (they assert) that B does not necessarily follow A with any degree of certainty. Children's day-to-day experience is non-linear. In short, things are messy, and schools which try to control events as if everything could be planned and ordered are increasingly outdated. Trying to organise learning in controlled packages and thinking of children as units misses the point. Lesson bells do not define learning. It is not confined to classrooms. Seeking to manage student behaviour in isolation from the rest of school life is to miss the point entirely. Schools are not cultural vacuums; the dominant culture has to be one that places learning at the fore. Learning has to dominate the way in which children are taught. How children are taught has to be central to the way in which the members of the organisation interact together. To see a distinction between the learning outcomes and the behavioural outcomes is to miss an opportunity.

The purpose of this extended discussion of the role of the deputy head is to show that when you apply to be a school leader, it is important to know what kind of leader you want to be. To do this, you need to have considered what constitutes leadership and thought about the function of schooling and education as a whole. Handy (1995) asserted that those who think the unthinkable will shape the future; to shape the future, you need, first of all, to think.

Back to the interview

Some people enjoy interviews; it brings out the best in them. In the case of a deputy headteacher, the interview does set the scene for your future work in the school. If it is a good interview where you are able to articulate your views and explain what you think, then it is probable that the job is right for you. If you feel uncomfortable, if the vibes are wrong, then it probably isn't.

If all this sounds rather vague and has an air of inevitability, then that is deliberate. Morgan (1992) listed, in rank order, the criteria declared by selectors in three LEA secondary headship appointments as:

1 Personality
2 Experience
3 Answers to questions
4 Qualifications
5 Appearance/voice/presence
6 Local culture knowledge
7 Educational philosophy
8 Liberal outlook
9 Previous performance
10 Community concern

The dominant criterion of personality raises perhaps more far-reaching questions than any other. It appears, from Morgan's research, that the selection process is largely about the search for the 'right' personality. The danger, of course, is that it may come to be about social acceptability more than about future job performance. A management perspective, concerned as it is with the achievement of explicit objectives, is unequivocal: job selection must be viewed as a procedure concerned with predicting future job performance and ensuring that the criteria the selection procedure uses have predictive validity.

To redress the balance, in response to the inadequacies of the traditional interview methods with their emphasis on image factors, there has been a movement towards the assessment centre approach (discussed in Chapter 4). This approach concentrates heavily on the specific skill dimensions of the role and aims to assess them by a range of tests and exercises, as well as structured interviews.

It is important to note that many schools have moved a long way towards this more assessment-centred model; however, the rider to all this is that working in a school, especially at a senior level, is about working with people. The human dimension, which is laid bare by the selection process, is both its strength and its weakness.

Summing up

The business of applying for the post of deputy headteacher is time consuming both for the individuals who apply and for the schools which recruit. The appointment is always very important to a school because of the significant role that the deputy head will play in the future success of the organisation. The appointment will also be crucial to the future career of the successful candidate, who will experience at first hand how diverse the post can be, demanding a wide range of skills and considerable dedication and commitment. For these reasons the headteacher will need to be sure that the person appointed will be a colleague who adds value to the work of the team and has the highest principles and great integrity. All this takes time and the selection process is designed for both the applicant and the school to see whether they fit one another's specification.

As an aspiring deputy, you need to have thought about a huge range of issues, including the personal vision for education. This is of crucial importance because it will determine your philosophy of teaching and learning, and in consequence how you will lead and manage.

Action points

- Read all the information on the post and the school carefully. Make sure that you understand what you need to do and when.
- Consider whether your skills and attributes fit the profile of the person being sought.
- Think through your vision for education: what implication does this have for the way in which a school is managed and led?
- What does it mean to be a leader of the school of the future?
- What are the strengths of the school?
- What are its weaknesses?
- Who are the stakeholders of the school?
- Does this fit in with the type of school you want to be part of?
- Do you agree with the pastoral/curriculum model of deputy headship?
- Link your skills to the person and job specifications.
- At interview, be yourself – don't try to second guess what is required.
- Ask yourself seriously whether this job at this school is the one for you.
- Consider your long-term future in schools.
- Remember the process is designed to assess your capability to do this particular post in this school. A rejection is in this context.
- When you succeed, the feeling will be fantastic.

References and suggestions for further reading

Bowring-Carr C. and West-Burnham J. (1997) *Effective Learning in Schools* Pearson, London

Handy C. (1995) *The Age of Unreason* Arrow, London

Marland M. (1985) 'Pastoral Needs in Schools' in Lang P. and Marland M. (eds) *New Directions in Pastoral Care* Basil Blackwell, Oxford

Morgan C. (1992) 'Inside the Interview "Black Box": the Tenuous Status of Job-related Evidence in LEA Selection Panel Decisions' in Riches C. and Morgan C. (eds) *Human Resource Management in Education* Open University Press, Milton Keynes

Noble T. and Pym B. (1970) 'Collegial Authority and the Receding Locus of Power' in Bush T. (ed.) *Managing Education: Theory and Practice* Open University Press, Milton Keynes

Sundstrom E., Demeuse K.P. and Futrell D. (1990) 'Work-teams; Applications and Effectiveness' *American Psychologist*, **45**, 120–33

Weber M. (1947) 'Legal Authority in a Bureaucracy' in Bush T. (ed.) *Managing Education: Theory and Practice* Open University Press, Milton Keynes

3 Starting out

Tuesday, 2 December

Things to do today:

1 Before visiting new school tomorrow, continue preparations for new post.
2 Set work for my classes to do tomorrow — now that my successor has been appointed I can tell the classes that I'm leaving.
3 List of things I need to take/collect tomorrow:
   a timetable
   b analysis of 'Business excellence model'
   c proposals for the options process
   d notes from meetings with heads of departments at last visit
   e Paper on assessment — this is something that I need to start work on very soon
   f arrangements for the first day?
   g term dates
4 Going to miss the assessment meeting at school because I'll be out — send apologies.

Thinking about tomorrow — very excited. My last visit was really busy! I'll need to spend some time in the staffroom this time as I had a few meetings with staff but not in any social sense.

I'll miss the assessment meeting tomorrow at my current school. I've put a lot of work into this over the past two years and I'm leaving it at a critical stage — but surely the measure of how good the work has been will be the extent to which it continues after I leave.

This time is difficult. I still feel part of this school but I am less interested in what its future will be. Also, my opinion seems to be less important! There's no point asking me what I think should happen next term because I won't be there to make it so! Also, I want to move on. There's a mixture of emotions.

I've written a paper on assessment, one of the areas that I am most interested in. Looking at this model — it's very ambitious! I sent a copy to the head at Matthew Arnold last week and we'll be talking about it tomorrow I think.

Just want to get on with the job now.

When you are appointed to the job of deputy headteacher, it is difficult to explain the euphoria you feel. From discussions with colleagues it is clear that the process of applying to be a deputy head is, in many ways, one of the more difficult and trying challenges that you will encounter as a career teacher. There are a number of reasons for this; firstly, the competition is usually very fierce: you are competing against the full range of experiences (rather than, say, only English teachers applying for a head of English post); secondly, getting the job is very much about the personal relationship between the applicant and the senior team. When the phrase 'fitting in' is used, it suggests that the candidate isn't going to change things and so it sounds rather dull. But the nature of the relationships in the senior team are necessarily close. The team will spend a great deal of time together and will work together in such a way that they can speak as one. In that respect, the business of applying for the post is quite trying. There may be nothing wrong with your application, or your interview, or anything, but you are disappointed. The relationship with the head-teacher will be a natural one in that early stage and the things that you want to do will be in keeping with what is required. Thirdly, the range of skills and experiences required are incredibly diverse and do tend to vary according to the school. A school with serious weaknesses may need a person with a high level of experience of the management of change; a school that has become somewhat stagnant could want a highly creative individual. So much of this depends on the particular characteristics of the school, the existing team and the applicants.

One of the features of school life is that you are appointed to a post several months before you actually start work on it. After the initial celebrations the old job still remains to be done while preparations for moving to the new one have to be made. This can be a cause of some disquiet. As a senior member of staff, you are used to having a major role in the school, but preparations have to be made for your successor. As time goes by, the discussions about the coming term, which herald the end of the current one, become of little importance to you. Indeed, because you are to have no part in what happens in the future, your views may no longer be sought. This can be a difficult time. After having felt total involvement with my school for five years I had to move to accept that I had no stake in its future. This was part of the distance I had to create between my past and my future.

Visiting the school for the first time after being appointed

Visiting the new school for the first time can be a nervous occasion. Between the time when you are appointed and when you first visit the school, you have probably had the opportunity for contact by telephone. However, as time goes on there comes a need to meet, at least with the headteacher, to draw up an agenda for the first term's work. Some people will be able to take this uncertainty in their stride; indeed, you could suggest that the ability to cope with these feelings is an essential part of the job, because so much of what happens during a typical day is uncertain and, in the first few weeks at least, unpredictable.

Visiting the school for the first time, then, is an important stage. At this visit, you are the deputy head, and even if someone else is in post, most teachers will treat you as the deputy head. This is quite a nice time. After all, to reach this position has taken considerable commitment to the profession and a high level of sustained, hard work. To be treated as an important person (because that is certainly what you are) is rewarding. In some cases the students at the school will know who you are, in others they may not. This can make you vulnerable: when you move around a school, you probably witness incidents of the usual kind – the hustle and bustle that accompanies large groups of young people as they move around their campus. A teacher has to respond to these happenings but until you are in post, there is a difficulty in dealing with children to whom you are unknown. However, to ignore misbehaviour might be seen as a sign of weakness – by staff and students alike.

You also need to familiarise yourself with the geography of the school. A good source of information is the material sent before the interview process. If it has got lost, then it is good advice to have it sent to you, so that you can familiarise yourself with basic information such as:

- the plan of the school
- the school day – lessons and timings
- where to park
- names of key people (it is surprising how quickly you can learn people's names when you have spent time learning their job roles: someone will say 'I'm . . .' and it will help a good deal if you can say, 'Ah yes, and you teach Geography')

The first visit is often characterised by a programme of meetings where you will discuss a wide range of curriculum issues, from the role of ICT in the school to behaviour management. Deciding what to say in these circumstances can be difficult, not becuase you do not have a view on these issues but it is generally felt that you have to get to know the people and the organisation before being in a position to make strategic change. It is good advice to take detailed notes during these early meetings: the organisation is new, every-thing is new, and it is vital that you retain as much information as possible. People will usually be polite and friendly but in some cases there will be reserve, a sense that you are not one of them. This was an important realisation for me. Having been a member of a teaching staff for so long, and having been able to interact with my colleagues on a personal level on most topics, I became conscious of the reserve that people now held me in. I responded with guarded remarks. A division was there.

At one meeting, a teacher was seeking my opinion on the assess-ment of Year 10. I have strong views on assessment policy; that was clear in my application. But as I started to speak there was a growing sense that my proposals would be seen as radical (I thought them proactive) and the comment made was, 'It's up to you, tell me what you want to happen'.

Until this point, I have been used to negotiating the changes I was making and having to weave my way through the diversity of opinion that had characterised the subject team I have led. It was, of course, entirely possible for me, as a head of Mathematics, to impose a policy and ensure its implementation. However, school management is subtler than that. Leading a team of teachers is about changing hearts and minds. While it is possible, by force of personality, to force through an issue, it does not change the mindset of those who have to implement the policy – the policy, of course, being designed to change the educational experiences of young people. Was this comment by this teacher a sign of his deference to me, as deputy head? Was this assertion symbolic of the management style operating in the school? Or was he testing me out to see what my modus operandi would be?

It was necessary for me to reflect on these questions at this stage. If the comment was intended to be deferential, then, in a sense, that was very nice. One of my motivations was to have power and authority. I wanted the status that goes with the role. On my first visit to the school, at this superficial level, I was being treated as someone of importance. However, if it was a sign of deference, it perhaps obscured the management stresses that would be implied. If the senior staff (or indeed any of the staff) were deferential to the deputy head, then there was a tacit expectation that the deputy head would know what to do. Further, there is a presumption that the deputy head has clarity of vision and has thought through all the implications of a decision in order to have reached the point of being able to articulate what needs to be done and what should happen.

There are dangers inherent in this view. There is no doubt that leadership demands clarity of purpose and strength of vision. The leaders of the school need to have thought through the issues that will affect and determine the organisation's direction. This is part of creating an organisational culture which reflects the aims of the school. However, this cannot take place in a vacuum. It cannot be done quickly. It takes time, effort and a commitment to debate and deliberation. It is certainly not to be undertaken hastily, and definitely not in the first few hours.

If, however, the statement was a sign of the management style in the school, then there was a lot of thinking to be done. If the management style in the school was that policy was determined by the Senior Management Team (SMT) and then imposed on the rest of the staff, then it would be at variance with my model of school management and leadership. To impose policy on a group of teachers, thereby disenfranchising them, was, in my view, a dangerous strategy and not one that would lead to sustainable school improvement. Fullan and Hargreaves (1992) argue that too often there is a gap between 'leaders and led'. Their assertion is that where responsibility is left solely to formal leaders, it overloads them, resulting in incorrect and frequently imposed solutions. This system also fails to prepare younger teachers for future leadership roles. Therefore, a system which imposes management solutions was contrary to my model of school leadership.

The alternative course for the junior teacher was to test me out, to see what I had to offer and whether my ideas were workable and reasonable. We all feel the need to assess newcomers and see where they might fit into the existing structures. For the deputy head this is an important issue to consider. Do you see yourself as one of the staff or do you ally yourself with the headteacher? At this stage, because I did not know any of the people well, my allegiance could only be to the role. The rest would come later.

This first visit passed in a succession of meetings. I spent a long time listening to people. I think this was the right thing to do. I wrote down practically everything that was said to me. This gave me the opportunity to reflect on what had been said to me later.

There was a sense of displacement, however, and a surreal quality to the task that lay ahead.

I made a subsequent visit to the school, in line with my agenda. I wanted time to find my way around and to discuss my teaching commitment in detail with heads of departments. When preparing for the meetings with heads of departments to discuss my teaching, I was conscious of the role I was to take on. As a head of Mathematics, I had worked with two other senior members of staff who had both been heads of Mathematics. On occasion they made comments beginning 'When I was a head of Mathematics I . . .' This was sometimes helpful (which I'm sure was the intention) but I had my own vision for the subject and the team. However, as deputy head, I did not want to give the impression that I was out to usurp the role of head of department. This is a cause for reflection on the nature of the role of deputy head. Because of the teaching commitment (typically 25–50 per cent of the timetable), you are in a sense still a teacher; however, the remit of the job differs considerably from that of the classroom teacher. If, for example, you accept the work of the team in the manner of a main-scale teacher and adopt that kind of role, then you are open to the charge of condoning the work being done, of not influencing strongly and the like. Yet to be a fundamental and pivotal part of the subject team, while valuable to that particular area, will be to the detriment of other parts of the school. There is no easy answer to this. You must ensure that your own subject area is not treated more favourably than any other. You must provide challenge and support to all curriculum areas. Moreover, this illustrates the conflicting roles that a new deputy head has to reconcile. It is too easy to involve yourself in the work of a subject team; if you have come through the head of department route, that is where your expertise lies. But this may be avoiding the fundamental challenge for the new deputy head: how to make the transition to your new role (in my case, from subject leader to school leader).

The time passed quickly between this visit and the start of the new term. The holiday was a curious one: I felt that I should be doing something. After all, I was about to take on a challenging role in an organisation that needed a lot of my attention. But the loose ends from my last school had been tied up and there was little I could do productively and usefully to prepare for the new job. However, the things I did do were of tremendous use: I learned the names and job roles of the teachers in my new school and did detailed preparation for the classes I was to teach.

By this time I had met most of the staff, but under circumstances which made it difficult to remember their names and jobs. However, after taking a staff list and learning the names of the teachers and the subjects they taught and the responsibilities they held, when I came to meet them again, I was able to make the link between the name on the list and the individual.

Preparing the lessons I was to teach was to be a huge benefit over the coming weeks. To go from teaching 80 per cent of the time to something approaching 30 per cent of the week sounds feeble. However, as the days unfolded, there seemed to be no opportunity to prepare for classes and so the security of my lesson plans was a source of comfort.

First day tomorrow – a staff training day. There's a slight irony in that probably the only person who needs training is I! I think that I am the only new member of staff joining the school tomorrow. I have discussed my first day with the head and I think it will be OK to spend time getting organised.

There are some whole-staff activities organised – on the subject of behaviour management – so I'll probably join a group to discuss this.

The first day

My first day as deputy head was uneventful in many ways. But what did I expect? I drove to the new school and as I walked through the building towards my newly decorated office, I was conscious of having a huge job description but nothing to do. The first day of term was a staff training day. The programme had been set out, and I had no role in its preparation or delivery. This was deliberate. The headteacher had said that in the early days he didn't want me to be 'under pressure' – that was to come soon enough. Therefore, on that first day, I was to be introduced to the staff formally – but what would I say? It would be nice to say something profound.

Over the holidays I had been reading the memoirs of John Major. He recalled his first speech as Prime Minister, after accepting the invitation from the Queen.

> As I began the drive back down the Mall, I wondered about what I would say to the media waiting in Downing Street. On a scrap of paper I set out some of the things that I believed: my hopes of creating a nation at ease with itself. . . . perfidious thoughts, no doubt, but deeply felt . . .
>
> 'I don't promise you that it will be easy, and I don't promise you that it will be quick, but I believe it to be an immensely worthwhile job to do. Because it will be neither easy nor quick – if you will forgive me – I will go into Number 10 straight away and make a start right now.'

I was not going to be Prime Minister – or even headteacher – but these words resonated through my mind as I prepared to take on the challenges that lay ahead. In the end I took the advice of the headteacher. I simply said, 'Good morning, everyone' – the rest was to follow.

This staff training day presented another important point, however. Part of the time was spent working in subject teams. When everyone arose to move to their respective areas, I became aware that I had nowhere to go – or, more particularly, no one to go with. Having spent the past ten years identified closely with a subject team, I was suddenly without a group of colleagues with whom I would spend my time. Fortunately, the headteacher came to my rescue and we had one of our many meetings on the myriad topics to be covered over the next few months.

Fullan and Hargreaves (1982) describe teaching as 'a lonely profession', which is often seen as pejorative. New teachers have to learn to cope with the children in the classes they teach. While they have the support of the others around them, for the period of time that the school defines as a lesson, they are, for the most part, on their own. As they develop strategies for dealing with the issues that arise during the course of the teaching day, they become, of necessity, autonomous. Fullan and Hargreaves argue that it is this professional isolation which limits access to new ideas and better solutions, and drives stress inward to fester and accumulate.

In teaching, however, this isolation is a characteristic trait rather than a personality weakness. The construction of the school day and the nature of teaching necessitate it. To suggest that it is an inevitable consequence of the education construct is to miss the point. As deputy head, I might perhaps become more isolated from the business of teaching. My work could turn out to confine me to my office, letting me interact only with a small group of people. A more radical approach to the role would be required if my agenda was to increase collaboration and create cohesion.

The management of education has often been seen as causing this isolationism and malaise. Bowring-Carr and West-Burnham (1997) reflect on the nature of schooling and set out their vision of tomorrow's school. They write of schooling today:

> Not too many years ago, there was the ludicrous situation that schools, expensive buildings with expensive resources, sat idle for about two months in the summer . . . schools are facing a number of paradoxes and challenges. An organisation that is geared to enabling teachers to teach, and is not based on the multiple ways in which children learn.

This was the challenge that I saw before me. How to transform this organisation into a learning culture? How to put the philosophy I had built up over a number of years into practice? Until this point, my philosophy of education had its basis in Mathematics; now it had to develop across the curriculum and engage others in its evolution. This was to be my challenge.

The second day

The next day dawned and the students were to return to school. I had two lessons to teach and I was also to speak at the school assembly. Planning the first lessons with a new class is always difficult. My concern was to make sure that the lessons I taught were of the highest standard. My job description included responsibility for the quality of teaching and learning, so I was conscious that my lessons at least had to meet the highest standards.

I reflected on previous moves in my career. For the most part, the jobs I have held have been curriculum based. I had been a class teacher and subject leader, and also a year head. The authority I held in all of the roles (though to a lesser extent as head of year) came from my expertise in the classroom. My authority and status among students in the school came from the fact that I had taught a good number of them over the course of the time I was in post. For those who were not taught by me, I was the head of Mathematics who saw them going to Mathematics lessons, and talked to their teachers about their work in Mathematics. I was a very visible person. Further, the gossip network of schools is such that a teacher's reputation spreads quickly and any challenging interactions with students tend to permeate the school community. I was a well-respected head of Mathematics whose authority had grown from classroom practice. As deputy head, I would need to find other ways of developing a reputation and creating a power base.

If you have been promoted within the school, you need to think through your role very carefully. There are many advantages; there is no problem of unfamiliarity as you will know the staff and students well. It is also likely that you will have become more involved in the relevant discussions during the weeks before you start your new appointment. However, you are moving to a position where you may have to support a policy you previously criticised. The nature of Senior Management Teams can be likened to that of Cabinet: the decision of the Cabinet is the decision of everyone. In many ways the response to this situation has to be the same for all new deputies: concentrate on doing the job in the right way; be a person who acts with integrity at all times. This makes the transition possible. The stressors are different but they cannot be underestimated.

Coping with new situations

The range of things that the deputy headteacher has to deal with is considerable. The first few days can be very stressful because you will have to deal with matters outside your previous experience. Below is a list of things that can happen during the working day of a deputy headteacher:

- you have to lead staff morning briefing
- you are on general patrol at lunchtime
- you have to write a job description
- you have to prepare an agenda for a heads of departments meeting
- you have to co-ordinate Form 7
- you have to deal with a parental complaint
- you have to decide how many ties to order for the next year
- Year 11 reports are due to be written – you are line manager for the reporting system
- there is a problem with a SIMS module you haven't used before
- there is disagreement about whether a grade or a percentage should be recorded on the school reports
- you notice that a lot of the girls are wearing jewellery, which is forbidden by school rules
- the headteacher goes to a meeting out of school and the fire alarm sounds

Clearly such a list is not exhaustive and is set down to illustrate the range of issues that the deputy headteacher has to deal with and is expected to be able to respond to at any time. The range of tasks does say something about the enormity of the job. Most schools hold some kind of meeting, perhaps daily or a few times during the week. Its purpose is to give staff reminders or to tell them about concerns, etc. Moreover, it is also an important means of creating and sustaining the whole staff dynamic: teaching can be an isolated and isolating job and opportunities for the whole teaching group to come together are therefore important. For the headteacher or (in my case) his deputy, this meeting forms part of the dynamic that is school leadership.

I have discussed being on duty at lunchtime, one of the items on the list, with a deputy head colleague. Lyn said that she found being on duty at lunchtime was one of the most important things she did. It gave her the opportunity to be seen by the whole school and respond to particular issues. I know from my previous experience that when I was on duty I would see students and could have a quick word with them, praising them for their work or reminding them of my expectations. Such informality can be useful, and as deputy head I have to be aware of this. Sending for someone to discuss a particular issue raises the stakes but the informal word can be very effective.

A particular factor during these first few days is, of course, that in a new job you want to do your best and to make a good impression. We all make mistakes, we all get things wrong, but we don't want to do it during our first few days on the job. As deputy headteacher, you do feel exposed, and this is really where you part company with the teaching staff. Teachers expect the senior team to know what to do. They expect them to be able to advise and help. If someone comes to you with a problem, as deputy head-teacher you should know what to do. That is the received wisdom. As a newly appointed deputy headteacher, of course you want to help, to do things, to sort things out. However, much caution needs to be exercised during the first few weeks. Just as 'you only get one chance to make a first impression', there is only one set of 'first few days'. Teachers are, in the main, kindly people and they respond better to an admission that you don't know what to do or a request for help than to someone rushing in and getting it spectacularly wrong. We all know this, but in the heat of the moment when you feel vulnerable and expectations are high, it is easy to forget the basics.

Hopefully, not all the events listed above will happen on the same day, or even during the first week, but it is worthwhile reflecting on some of these matters as preparation for the first few days and weeks.

Firstly, what do you do if the headteacher is absent? This is particularly pressing if you are the sole deputy. There are, of course, a number of reasons why he or she might be absent and the advice also depends on the length of the absence. However, it is important to discuss with the headteacher what is expected of you in this eventuality. Things to clarify are:

- dealing with the post
- what to do in an emergency
- procedures for exclusion (if the policy is that only the headteacher or deputy headteacher can exclude)

Of course, much of this depends on the nature and duration of the absence. If it is short and was known in advance, then it is much simpler; in many cases the absence is for a few hours and things can be 'held' until the headteacher returns. If the absence is longer, agreement needs to be reached on matters such as: where the deputy headteacher is to work (possibly from the headteacher's office, with the secretary); what is the procedure for decision making; whether you have authority to sign, etc. It is important that, as a newly appointed deputy, you are always able to contact the headteacher; being left in charge of the school for the first few times can be daunting, and confidence will grow from knowing what to do and how to respond. I think that most headteachers would prefer their deputy to contact them if in doubt rather than presume that their chosen action is the right one. Some judgement needs to be exercised here; you are an accomplished professional, but the major factor is inexperience.

Secondly, what do you do when asked for policy decisions? One of the things that characterises the role of headteacher is that everything they say is school policy. As leaders of their schools, their utterances show how they want the school to run. The new deputy headteacher has to learn what the headteacher's views are on matters and to reach agreement on how to implement them. This is not to assert that the deputy headteacher is a conduit for the headteacher's wishes. Rather, it illustrates the need to spend time getting to know the headteacher in order to make responses in line with his or her wishes. It is vital for the smooth running of any school that there is clarity of purpose on major policy matters; as the new deputy headteacher, you are well advised to defer any comment until time has been found for discussions with senior colleagues.

What is very important in the first few weeks is to accept your inexperience in the role. This is quite hard because the deputy headteacher is necessarily an experienced teacher. However, the range of things that present themselves is such that it can be important to seek advice; in most cases this will be from the head-teacher and other senior colleagues. In another context Brighouse and Woods (1999) describe the pitfalls that await the unwary. They describe the 'doubtful' benefits of previous experience. There will obviously be tasks that you have undertaken in the previous post that you have to repeat in the new school. It is easy to think that because it worked in one school, it will work in another. The issue of difficult students is perhaps a good example; as an experienced teacher, you develop strategies for dealing with the most difficult students. It is often easier to work with them if you've known them since they were 11 (or 5, or 13, depending on the type of school). As a teacher, you develop a 'history' with your students. Conse-quently, in the face of a difficult situation you are able to draw on that reserve as they get older. Unfortunately, as deputy headteacher you are often called on to deal with such students but at first there is no history, and so the complex negotiations that are possible with a recalcitrant student are doomed to failure. For the most challenging students, the authority and power of the office are worth little. An experienced teacher finds this hard to appreciate. We forget, as time goes on, how long it takes to build up the 'history'. In the context of school leadership, Brighouse and Woods (1999) recall a female head commencing a second headship: 'You forget what it means to be unknown. You take short cuts which you could get away with in the last place.'

Hard though this may be, there is no short cut to getting yourself known in the school. Staff and students will know who you are but this will not necessarily help you to deal with a situation; at worst it will make you more anxious if you are unsure what to do.

As I commented earlier, I was introduced to the students at the whole school assembly. I assumed that everyone would then know who I was. However, a week later I was teaching a class where I observed a student wearing a ring. I asked her to take it off and she refused. She told me that it was her engagement ring and that she wasn't going to take it off. Further, she said that if I wanted to send her to Mrs Brown (the previous deputy head), then that was OK. In the ensuing discussion, it was clear that despite attending the school assembly, she didn't know that Mrs Brown had left and that I was now the deputy head. In retrospect, these incidents are amusing but they illustrate the dangers of presumption; we cannot presume that our status, the sign on the door, will cut any ice with either students or staff. Just as we had to prove ourselves and establish our authority in our other roles, we have to do so again. Further, we have to reflect on these incidents and see them for what they are; the issue here is not that the girl refused to obey the deputy headteacher, but how the matter was resolved. If I had taken the authoritative line, then I might have won the day, but lost some face. By tackling it in a quiet, calm way, and noting that she clearly didn't know who I was, the matter was resolved and my authority took one small step forward.

Summing up

Your first few weeks as deputy head are a challenge, owing to the enormity of the task and the effect of being, in a sense, deskilled. What makes the transition possible is the ability to translate core competencies into the new situation. Further, there is a need to have a philosophy of school leadership; this will be challenged as the days pass, but the principles of leadership are ones which underpin all the actions that you take and the matters you decide.

Action points

- Allow the head to determine your agenda for the first day. This gives you an insight into the likely priorities for your work.
- Prepare for the meetings by compiling a list of questions you might ask. These might be of the 'How has your job changed over the past year?' type. They are good 'ice-breakers'.
- Take notes on the conversations that you have. This will be valuable later as you reflect on the day.
- Don't agree to things! The motto 'If you want a decision today, it's no' may seem a little harsh, but it is better to say this than to agree to something you will later regret.
- On subsequent visits, if possible, organise your teaching. Make sure you have the textbooks, schemes of work, class lists, a timetable, etc.
- Spend time planning lessons for the first half term. Produce the resources that you will need. This will enable you to focus on the new parts of your job, and still teach high-quality lessons.
- Spend time with the headteacher and determine the focus for your first few days and weeks.
- It is important to make a positive impression, but there is a need to 'grow' into the role. This will take time and you have to expect this.

References and suggestions for further reading

Begley P. (ed.) (1999) *The Value of Educational Administration: a Book of Readings* RoutledgeFalmer, London
In this book the values and ethics that underpin educational management are examined.
Boler M. (1999) *Feeling Power: Emotions and Education* Routledge-Falmer, London

This book focuses on the ways emotions are conceived and enacted in educational settings.

Bowring-Carr C. and West-Burnham J. (1997) *Effective Learning in Schools* Pearson, London

Brighouse T. and Woods D. (1999) *How to Improve Your School* Routledge, London

Fullan M. and Hargreaves A. (1992) *What's worth fighting for in your school* Open University Press, Buckingham

Gold A. and Evans J. (1999) *Reflecting on School Management* RoutledgeFalmer, London
In this book the various issues related to management are teased out and a selection of ideas and pragmatic solutions informing good practice are examined.

Major J. (1999) *The Autobiography* HarperCollins, London

4 Assessing the motivated: issues over recruitment?

Wednesday, 11 March

Things to do today:
1   Write advert for the senior teacher.
2   Write job description
3   Write person specification.

Recruiting people to join our school is a worry. I don't doubt that we will get a lot of good applicants but how do we ensure that we select the right people for interview? Further, once we've invited colleagues for interview how are we going to select the best person?

And what is it that we want from this person? Some of the characteristics we will want:

• excellent teacher
• excellent facilitator of meetings
• needs to be able to manage a budget
• be part of the leadership group – needs to fit in with the existing team and add that 'something'

Thing is, as I start to think about this I'm increasingly convinced that the traditional model of teacher recruitment isn't good enough. We read someone's letter, invite them for interview, ask them some questions and then decide – bit simplistic, but that's about it. The success of the appointment depends on the quality of the questioning technique. But unless everyone is good at this then we could make a mistake.

If we get it wrong we've committed the school's resources in a way that won't move us forward.

I think that there are other ways of assessing people's suitability for the jobs we offer. That's really the key – it is about assessing the potential of others to do the job. To do this we'll have to really think hard about what we want from this person and then design the recruiting process around the job they will do. So we will need to think about:

- person specification – qualifications, experiences, previous roles, etc.
- job specification – what we want them to do, how will we know if they've done the job well, etc.
- are there other ways we can select – psychometrics, presentations, role plays, how people behave?
- how all the senior team, the governors and others on the staff can be involved

The recruitment of teachers is very predictable; it is largely about interviews and seeing what people are like. This is perhaps rather harsh, but all those involved in the recruitment of the teaching staff need to consider the issues of recruitment.

The task of teaching has grown considerably in its levels of complexity. The dynamic of educational change is considerable; there is a good deal of research being undertaken in many places on such topics as learning, teaching, school leadership, value-added, statistics, etc. This research is not only being carried out in the universities in this country; there is an international dimension too. Add to this the growth of action research projects that are being carried out in many schools by practising teachers, and the picture becomes a very full one.

More and more is demanded of us all. 'More of the same only better' and, if possible, for more people. This was the comfortable view of change that permitted those in the 1960s and 1970s to reconcile themselves with their own personal prosperity. It allowed the big to grow bigger (in terms of industry, recall the growth of the car manufacturing giants). Associated with this was the rise of powerful industrial magnates, people who controlled very large organisations with considerable personal and industrial strength.

This could not be sustained. The experience of the 1980s which saw massive increases in people's personal wealth – the whole business of power-dressing, Porsche-driving yuppies (young upwardly-mobile professional people) and dinkies (double income no kiddies) – could not be sustained for ever.

It is not just that the pace of change has speeded up, although we are all aware that it has. The ownership of such things as personal computers is a particularly good example. You may remember the launch of the Sinclair ZX81 – a full 1K of memory on sale at Christmas time for £99 – or BBC computers, with 32K of memory – a lot for a home computer – which were used widely in schools. Today, we have considerable computer technology at our fingertips, so much so that this book will be available on-line. But long before it reaches the shelves (and the virtual equivalent), it will have been emailed to the publishers and only when it reaches the final manuscript stage will it exist in hard-copy form.

Faster change is alright when it leads to 'more only better' schools. However, when the associated improvement places ever-increasing demands on people, then perhaps we need to think through what we want from our staff.

The headteacher and the deputy will normally be involved in staff appointments. There are some organisations where this varies. Recently, I was discussing staff recruitment with a deputy colleague; at her school the appointment of all junior staff (defined as those with less than two management points) had been delegated to her. This is quite unusual. More often the appointing process is shared, and so it should be. The staff are the school's greatest resource and the investment of time in the recruitment process is vital to secure the school's future. Get it right and the school rejoices in the mutual benefit that the best person brings; get it wrong and you can be stuck with an unsuitable person for a very long time.

The process of recruiting staff needs to be thought through. Selecting on the interview only can cause difficulties because it relies too much on people's honesty. References bear similar hazards. These traditional methods of staff selection have served us reasonably well for many years, but we have to ask ourselves whether they are fit for the purpose in the schools of the future.

There are a number of reasons why the interview process may be inadequate as the sole selection tool:

- it relies solely on the candidate's ability to present him- or herself to an interview panel (a situation that is false and does not relate to the daily task)
- the nature of school leadership requires an ability to interact at a variety of levels
- the nature of school leadership requires a facilitative as well as a presentational role
- there is a functional aspect that cannot be determined through interview situations

One outcome from all the research is a perceptible change in the level of understanding of school organisation. Indeed, the juxta-position of the two words 'school' and 'organisation' recognises the individual nature of school life. Comparisons have been made with business and industry, and attempts are often made to compare practices. With this has emerged a vocabulary that describes and attempts to explain these practices. For example, Handy (1991) compares the organisation of the past to that of the future. Organi-sations used to be perceived as gigantic pieces of engineering with largely interchangeable human parts. We talked of their structures and their systems, of inputs and outputs, of control devices and their management, as if the whole was one large factory. Today the language is not that of engineering but that of politics, with talk of cultures and networks, of teams and coalitions, of influence or power rather than control, of leadership, not management. What is required, therefore, is a new model to assess staff. We should be recruiting on the basis of the tasks that have to be done and should think through the ways in which we can assess people for these roles.

How do we assess? Through IQ?

There is good evidence to suggest that measures of general intelli-gence (so-called 'g') provide the single best predictor of professional success across jobs (e.g. Rees and Earles 1993, and Schmidt and Hunter, quoted in 1993 in Sternberg 1997). In a single analysis of the success in the full range of jobs in our society – engineers, office workers, care assistants, nurses and lawyers – conventional measures of intelligence would probably prove to be as good as, or better than, any other single measure. But measures that are highly predictive of success across jobs are not necessarily particularly predictive within jobs.

This is one reason why recruitment based on technical competence is not enough. The range of IQs across jobs is very large, whereas within jobs it may be relatively small. Sternberg (1997) illustrates this by comparing the IQ of an average assembly-line worker and an average actuary. This is likely to be larger than the difference in IQ between the top and bottom quartiles or possibly deciles within each of these jobs. By restricting the range of IQ, we lower the correlation across jobs.

Further, although IQ matters to some extent, it does not tell the whole story. Whatever your IQ, you will not succeed as a doctor, a watchmaker, an actuary or a teacher without a lot of knowledge about your area of specialisation. There is also the interpersonal element of the job: you will not succeed as a teacher unless you can explain things to people.

In addition, there is more to people than their IQ; their abilities cannot be measured solely in terms of their intelligence quotient. There is, of course more to the job of being a teacher, being a

---

This is where the difficulty of the job description and person specification arises. When we are recruiting, at whatever level, we are selecting someone who will be not only a teacher but a member of our team. The values of our organisation are the basis for everything we do and they drive all our systems and ways of working. We need people whose aims are concordant with our values – and that's the real test of any selection process.

subject leader, being a head of year than simply the application of intelligence. We need to think through what characteristics we seek and ensure that the measures we apply to those candidates guarantee that we recruit on the basis of what the job involves.

Beyond intelligence?

Sternberg (1997) suggests that we need to find measures that will predict job success in a way that goes beyond IQ. He describes the concept of 'tacit knowledge': the knowledge that you need to succeed in an endeavour, which is not formally taught or part of any formal discipline, and often not even verbalised although in theory it can be. It is knowledge that is typically acquired on the job or in the situation where it is actually used. It differs from more formal knowledge in that there is often resistance to its verbalisation. Sternberg uses the model of triarchic theory to explain how tacit knowledge is constructed. In the triarchic theory, a distinction is made between adaptation to existing environments, shaping of existing environments to transform them into different environments, and selection of wholly new environments. To put it simply, we change ourselves to suit our environment, we change our environment to suit ourselves, or we seek out a new environment that suits us better than our existing one.

Sternberg further categorises this form of knowledge. It is highly dependent on the particular job to which the tacit knowledge is applied. The taxonomy he proposes distinguishes between tacit knowledge about the self, others and tasks, on the one hand, and local versus global tacit knowledge, on the other.

Tacit knowledge about the self refers to knowledge about how to organise and motivate yourelf to work effectively. For example, knowing how to avoid procrastination could be an example of tacit knowledge about yourself. Tacit knowledge about others refers to knowledge about how to manage and get along with subordinates, colleagues of equal rank, and those in senior positions in the organisational hierarchy. Knowing what one can and cannot say to the headteacher is one example of tacit knowledge about others. Tacit knowledge about the job refers to how to get it done, for example being able to decide which textbook is most appropriate for a particular syllabus.

Local tacit knowledge is the kind that is used to get through the day: knowing what to do when a student hasn't completed the homework and failed to attend the lunchtime detention. Global tacit knowledge is used to make decisions that involve the career as a whole. Knowing when to move to another school for career advancement is an example.

Being a reflective practitioner is so important. I think in a way that has been something that I have had to think about a great deal. I don't just mean considering how I could do things better next time. Obviously if things don't work then it's necessary to take steps to ensure that it doesn't go wrong again. But when I talk things through with the head he encourages me to think not only about what I want to achieve but why it's important. In the discussions that follow I am challenged to consider my strategic goals and to reflect on the way I conduct myself and work with others.

Being self-aware — knowing what the impact of 'me' is on others — is crucial to the enactment of our values. It's not enough to believe in the values, they have to be seen to determine all that I do. Commitment to the values of our school is clearly important. Being a reflective practitioner is critical here.

Where does this leave us? What is being proposed is a new way of assessing the potential of people to do a job. When appointing a newly qualified teacher to the main scale a more conventional model may serve; but certainly, the criteria for assessing the suitability of a candidate for a middle-management role should be different, simply because the job itself is different.

Planning a recruitment day

Assessment centres

Assessment centres are often defined as 'a variety of testing techniques designed to allow candidates to demonstrate, under standardised conditions, the skills and abilities most essential for success in a given job'. Assessment centres are much more time consuming to develop and administer, require more people, and as a result cost more than traditional oral interviews. Why, then, has there been such a dramatic increase in their use? The answer is multidimensional. Firstly, the predictive validity and legal defensibility of unstructured oral interviews have been questioned for years. With the recent trend towards job-relevant testing, selection interviews have become more job-related and structured in format. This change has resulted in improved predictive validity, but generally the validity coefficients achieved are still not as high as those achieved with assessment centres.

Assessment centres allow candidates to demonstrate more of their skills through a number of job-relevant situations. Thus, assessors are able to observe candidates' effectiveness in a variety of realistic settings dealing with the typical issues and problems of the target job. The results are more accurate primarily because the test is more comprehensive and because the assessor can see how effective the candidate is, unlike the interview where the candidate has to convince the panel members orally. Interviews still have a place in the total selection process and are probably best utilised as the final step, at which the appointing panel can explore any issues raised during the assessment centre procedure.

Past performance may undoubtedly hold some value in predicting success. The problems that result from using it as a predictor usually revolve around measurement. Firstly, the conditions and requirements of your current job are often different from those of the senior one. Those new to deputy headship will recognise this fact readily. It is the case with teachers too: a person may be an excellent teacher, but possess only a few of the skills necessary for being an effective subject leader. Promotion on the basis of past performance alone means the school loses a good teacher and gains a poor head of department. In addition, the teacher would suffer a good deal in what could be a very painful and unnecessary transition.

Before setting up an assessment centre, it is important to think about what characteristics the organisation needs to see before it selects a candidate to join the staff. Perhaps, instead of thinking in terms of characteristics, we might think in terms of values. What values do our leaders need to have to make them effective people in our organisation? By considering what is desired, we can match activities to these values.

> We want our colleagues to be just that! We want them to work alongside others, sometimes to lead, sometimes to follow. Sometimes they will need to work alone but the best work is going to be when they collaborate with others. This is when the whole becomes greater than the sum of the parts. That is when we get committed and successful people who enjoy their work.

If we accept Sternberg's analysis of tacit knowledge, it can lead us to a new way of assessing people's potential. Sternberg proposes that assessors set out a range of scenarios which are job-related and job-specific. Then candidates rate their responses on a 1 (low) to 9 (high) scale. Some suggested scenarios are set out in boxes below.

Scenario 1: Managing yourself

You are concerned about your habit of putting off doing disagreeable tasks and you wish to improve this aspect of your work-related performance. Upon further examination, you find that it takes you much longer than your colleagues to mark a set of exercise books. You find it difficult to get down to starting to mark. You ask some of your colleagues who never seem to have this trouble for advice. Rate the quality of advice you are given:

- Wait to begin marking until you really have to do it (i.e. the night before you teach the class).
- Spend some time thinking just what it is you dislike about marking and try to change that aspect of it (i.e. having to work out a mark scheme).
- Get rid of all distractions (perhaps by taking the marking to a classroom somewhere) so that there is nothing to do except complete the marking.
- Force yourself to start the day by doing fifteen minutes' marking, in the hope that once you have started you will keep going.

The point to emphasise is that the way this model is applied is job-relevant and job-specific. By constructing scenarios for people to consider, we describe the job as it has to be done and the candidates have to consider their response. The scenarios in themselves do not really matter; they have to be plausible and relate to specific events in schools. That there are no 'objectively correct' answers is a strength. What is correct in one environment, for one person, might not be so elsewhere or for someone else. However, a real strength of these scenarios is that even if someone hasn't done the job of, say, head of department, the tests measure tacit knowledge acquired not only in a specific job, but also in life in general. They do not have to be administered in a paper-and-pencil format either. Simulations lend themselves to role plays and interview questions.

Scenario 2: Managing others

You have just learned that the headteacher has said that she requires detailed lesson plans from all the members of your subject team, to be submitted on Fridays ready for the next week. You have not been told why she has decided to introduce this monitoring process. It will involve teachers in a great deal of work and will be resisted strongly by them. Neither you nor any of the teachers at the school had any input into this decision, or into decisions about its format.

You are planning a team meeting to introduce your team to the new reporting procedures. Rate the quality of the following things you might do:

- Emphasise that you had nothing to do with the decision.
- Have a group discussion about the value of the new procedure and then put its adoption to a vote.
- Give your team details of how they can complain to the headteacher.
- Promise to represent their concerns faithfully to the headteacher but only after they have tried the new procedure for six weeks.
- Since you fear that the new procedure will get an unpleasant reaction, send them a memo and use the meeting for something else.
- Postpone the meeting until you find out the rationale for the new procedure.

Presented to the candidates as part of their preparation for an interview, Scenario 2 would enable the interviewer to explore their management and leadership potential. Most of us can think of a situation where the decisions of the senior team were 'directed' and some measure of unfavourable reaction followed.

Scenario 1 looked at the candidates' response to disagreeable tasks. The nature of work is such that in all jobs there are things we don't like to do but which have to be done. This scenario will enable the interviewers to key into the candidates' approach to these times and find out their response. Scenario 2 enables the interviewer to explore attitudes to authority and views on management styles.

An important part of any manager's work is using money and resources effectively and efficiently. Scenario 3 presents a situation where the candidate has to consider a number of pieces of information. At one level this scenario can be used to discuss financial protocol but at another level it can be used to explore candidates' attitudes to recommendation, personal knowledge and so on.

Scenario 3: Managing tasks

You are responsible for selecting the company which will provide technical support and new equipment for the computer system at school. You have narrowed the field to two contractors on the basis of their bids and, after further investigation, you are considering awarding the contract to Zippy Computers. Rate the following pieces of information in importance:

- The company has provided letters from other schools recommending its services.
- The Schools Computer Council reports no major complaints about this company.
- Zippy Computers' bid was £2,000 less than the other contractor's (approximate total cost of the work is £100,000).
- Former customers whom you have contacted strongly recommend Zippy Computers.

There are a number of other characteristics that you might look for when setting up an assessment centre and some of these are explored below.

Collegiality

Collegiality has been described as interaction between individuals characterised by honesty, trust, rapport and respect, a willingness to participate in group activities and collegial bonding (Cavanagh and Dellar 1996; Hargreaves 1994). Inasmuch as teachers have to interact with one another in this way, the ability to form relationships built on collegiality is essential for them.

The ability to prioritise work

One way to assess this characteristic is through the in-tray exercise described on p. 42. Candidates would be required to deal with the materials presented to them in a limited amount of time. Some assessors include material that is out of date to see if candidates notice. This seems rather underhand. There are better ways to see if candidates can attend to detail, for example asking them to analyse a budget statement or discuss a technical paper.

The advantage of this sort of exercise is that it is relatively easy to set up. However, if it is to be valid you need to decide what you are trying to find out. Some possible questions that this exercise could answer are shown in Table 4.1.

The in-tray exercise is useful in that it tests whether candidates can prioritise, but it can also be used to develop issues in a subsequent interview.

Compatibility

If teacher compatibility facilitates the collaboration process, then a shared philosophy about what constitutes learning is essential in the school. Collegiality can be fostered by shared beliefs about teaching and therefore it may be important to match team members in terms of these teaching beliefs. One way to assess this characteristic is through a *role-play exercise*. The candidate assumes the role of an incumbent of the post and must deal with a subordinate, an irate parent or a student about an issue, problem or complaint. It is important for the role player to be very well briefed and a very

Table 4.1 Linking questions, assessment centre evidence and the issues raised by the processes

Question	Evidence	Issues
Can the candidate do the work in the required time?	The candidate processes all the papers in the required time; this might be assessed through the priority order of the papers (i.e. numbering the papers).	• Is the task reasonable? • This makes no assessment of the quality of the decision-making process; this needs to be explored elsewhere.
Are the papers prioritised?	The assessor might sort the papers into the order he or she thinks is right and compare the candidates' response	• Again, without further exploration the reasons for the prioritisation might be lost. • Also, this 'marking' of candidates' responses could take a long time.
How does the person respond	Candidates could be asked to draft a letter in response to a paper from the pack	• Again the response would benefit from some discussion, or at least the criteria for a 'successful' letter would need to be considered in advance.

good actor. The interaction is observed and evaluated by the assessors. Depending on the problem, the issues can be explored in the interview. Examples of such a role play might include:

- dealing with a person in distress
- dealing with an intruder to the school premises
- responding to a phone call
- an interview with the press

Honesty and trust

Covey (1991) writes that we need to 'seek first to understand'. For Covey, the root cause of a lot of all problems to do with people is the basic communication problem: people do not listen with empathy. They listen from within their own personal experience. They lack the skill and attitude of empathy. The tenor of Covey's paradigm is that when people are living in harmony with their core values and principles, then they can be straightforward, honest and up-front. Trust determines the quality of the relationship between people. The question is how this can be evaluated in the assessment centre framework.

Brighouse and Woods (1999) describe the three types of friend that a school has:

- the 'hostile witness': someone who so disapproves of the running of the school that his or her involvement in its life has a bias towards negativity that is condemnatory
- the 'uncritical lover': someone who is so besotted with what he or she perceives as the all-embracing success of the school that the currency of praise is devalued by comments that are undifferentiatedly positive
- the 'critical friend': someone who understands and is sympathetic to the purpose of the school, knows its circumstances very well, is skilled in offering a second opinion, or sometimes a first opinion, about an issue only half perceived by the school itself or, if perceived, seen as impenetrable.

All schools would want the third of these types of friend. Some of the characteristics relating to the critical friend are reproduced in Table 4.2 with pointers towards interview technique.

Shared decision-making

If the successful candidate will have to lead a team (which characterises nearly all activity in schools) we need to recruit a person with the ability to do so. It is important to find out whether

Table 4.2 What does the interviewee's behaviour tell you?

Characteristic behaviour	Pointer during an interview
Asking questions which are increasingly focused, but speculative and not judgemental	The candidate understands that to find something out there needs to be a clear focus for enquiry and questions need to be raised. The candidate is prepared to speculate but not judge.
Using 'we' and 'us' rather than 'they'	Listen carefully to the candidate's response when asked questions about his or her current school. Is the language used inclusive, showing a sense of ownership of the work of the school?
When giving an opinion, sentences or questions are half-finished to preserve another's dignity	By asking questions about the school it is possible to assess to what extent the interviewee will be sensitive to the work of others.
Identifying personally and equally with their school's successes and failures	Ask about the projects candidates have been involved in. Do they identify strongly with them? Do you feel that they are telling you about what they have done personally or only about what others have done? Do they tell you about others with pleasure?
Seeing strengths as well as points for development	It is important for people to be able to judge what needs to be improved, but in a way that celebrates achievement and recognises effort and progress. Asking candidates what they would do differently if the work was repeated is one way to assess this characteristic.
Balancing 'appreciative enquiry' with 'problem solving'	Look for signs that people recognise the jobs that are to be done and are able to balance these against the successes the school has achieved.
Anticipating sensitivities	What is their response to the difficult situations? Do they recognise that certain things are embarrassing or sensitive?

people are capable of sharing the decision-making processes. One way to do this is to ask candidates to participate in *leaderless group discussion*. This exercise usually takes one of two forms. In the 'unassigned roles' or 'co-operative group discussion' candidates are given a number of current issues or problems and instructed to formulate specific recommendations or decisions. In the 'assigned roles' or 'competitive group' each candidate is given a different position or recommendation to support, and time to make a persuasive presentation to the other members of the group. Then, as in co-operative groups, candidates are expected to come to a consensus in the time allowed as to which position or recommendation should be adopted. The group's interaction is observed by an assessor team, each assessor paying particular attention to one or two of the candidates.

Examples of scenarios that might be considered are:

- recommending a course of action to deal with a budgetary situation
- deciding to award funds following a bidding process
- debating a curriculum innovation
- discussing a change to the school's status (e.g. specialist school status)

Facilitative leadership

Success in leading is as much contingent upon how you lead as it is on what you lead. Leadership can be highly subjective and there are many books to read on the subject. However, in this context it is appropriate to recall those characteristics listed by Born and Jansen (1997):

- leaders have a vision: they are able to formulate their goals and tasks in an idealistic way
- they have very strong belief in themselves
- leaders put very high demands on themselves and their employees: thus they are 'authoritarian' in the sense that they load the weight of their work-related tasks onto employees

- leaders are very strong communicators and so are able to inspire employees
- typical personal characteristics include 'compelling eyes'; often leaders are perceived as handsome

Some of these are interesting, particularly the final point: shall we only appoint good-looking people? Surely not!

One way to assess the potential of people as leaders is the *oral presentation exercise*. In this exercise candidates are allowed a brief time to plan, organise and prepare a presentation on an assigned topic to a specific audience. They then make the presentation and respond to questions and/or challenges. The assessors play the role of the audience.

Mentoring

Mentoring is emerging as one of the most powerful forms of intervention to raise levels of attainment. One way to assess a teacher's commitment to this kind of work is through an *observed coaching session*. The criteria for such an assessment could include the OfSTED lesson criteria. The one-to-one relationships between the teacher and the students, and the level of detail that is provided on the performance and identification of appropriate strategies to improve that performance, could also be evaluated.

Psychometric testing

One measure that is becoming increasingly popular is the psychometric test. A qualified person has to interpret the results of those regulated by the British Psychological Society. There are six main types of psychometric tests: intelligence tests, ability tests, aptitude and attainment tests, personality questionnaires, projective and objective tests of personality, interest and motivation tests. A full description and critique of the main tests used for selection purposes is found in Kline (1993).

In general, psychometric tests are the most valid method of assessment. Where valid tests exist, as in the fields of ability, motivation and personality, there is no point in trying to find other methods of assessment. Interviews, in the view of Kline (1993), simply add errors to selection procedures. The weight attached to psychological tests in the selection process should be determined empirically by their correlations with job success or their ability to discriminate the relevant occupational groups.

The organisation of an assessment centre will clearly depend on how many people are involved in the selection, the number of candidates and the activities selected. However, a number of pointers should be considered:

- starting the day: decide what time you want candidates to arrive; a brief meeting between each candidate and the head-teacher is recommended
- tour of the school: who is going to show the candidates around?
- selection activities: organise these so that candidates have enough to do but do not become exhausted and pressured
- allow time for them to have refreshments
- allow time for them to meet with other staff not involved in the selection process
- allow time for them to think
- organise the final interviews so that any candidate with a long distance to travel is interviewed first
- decide how will you inform candidates of the decision – by telephone?

Figure 4.1 gives an example of a recruitment day with the timings used.

What is the point of selection processes?

The objective in this selection procedure is to ensure that the school gets the right person for the job. As the deputy headteacher, you may find it difficult to judge this because of lack of experience in selection or lack of knowledge about the selection process. Relying on the interview alone has significant drawbacks; it is in many ways

Produce name badges for the candidates

Candidates

1 Mrs Julie Flower

2 Mr Robert Plant

3 Miss Suzanne Rose

4 Mr Victor Turf

5 Ms Jan Dill

6 Dr Louis Gold

Book the library – inform staff well in advance that the library will be closed

Organise students to take the candidates on the tour

8.30	Arrive and meet headteacher					
8.45–9.45	Observed leaderless group discussion and school tours					
	Each candidate is asked to lead a discussion on their selected topic					

Book venues and provide candidates with a map showing location of the toilets

Group Discussion 8.45–9.15
Venue: Library
Candidates 1, 2, 3

School tour 9.15–9.45
Candidates 1, 2, 3

School tour 8
Candidates 4, 5, 6

Group Discussion 9.15–9.45
Venue: Library
Candidates 4, 5, 6

Devise a means of recording outcomes to questions

	In-tray exercise	Interview with assistant head and head of year, venue: meeting room	Lesson observation and feedback session	In-tray exercise venue: A1	Interview with assistant head and head of year	Lesson observation and feedback session
9.45–10.15	Candidate 1	Candidate 3	Candidate 2	Candidate 4	Candidate 6	Candidate 5
10.15–10.45	Candidate 2	Candidate 1	Candidate 3	Candidate 5	Candidate 4	Candidate 6
10.45–11.05	Break in staffroom					

Who will organise this?

Arrange for someone to look after them during break

11.05–11.35	Candidate 3	Candidate 2	Candidate 1	Candidate 6	Candidate 5	Candidate 4
12.00	Final interviews commence. Candidates will be asked to deliver their 5 minute presentation at the start of the interview.					
12.00	Candidate 1					
12.30	Candidate 2					
1.00–1.30	Lunch					
1.30	Candidate 3					
2.00	Candidate 4					
2.30	Candidate 5					
3.00	Candidate 6					

This 25 minute slot is necessary for those who've been interviewing to let the panel know their views

At the end of the interview candidates are free to go. The decision will be communicated by telephone in the evening

During the day candidates are free to visit any classroom and coffee is available all day in the staffroom.

Please ask the headteacher's PA for anything you need. *Make sure the staff know this*

Observed discussion: the observers will be the headteacher, deputy headteacher and head of Science.

Lesson observation: this will be of a Year 7 lesson and the feedback will be observed by Dr Fred Bushy, Science adviser

Interview panel: headteacher, Mr R. Jones; deputy headteacher, Mrs S. Tranter; head of Science, Mr I. Newton; school governor, Mrs Jo Craig

Figure 4.1 Selection for head of Botany, 31 May

a defunct model when used on its own. However, when interviews are conducted carefully, and the issues at stake are explored, then of course candidates have to say what they really think. The point about using assessment centres – which is a collective term for a range of assessment activities – is that they enable the assessors to see the candidates in a variety of situations. In addition, mistakes are less likely to be made simply because you will know so much more about the candidates by seeing them in a variety of situations. It gives you a range of information.

This approach can also be used when assessing candidates for an internal promotion. The group profile from a promotional assessment centre is likely to give a picture of overall strengths and weaknesses within the classification assessed and provide insight into which aspects of an organisations' training programme to commend and which need revision. The individual candidate profiles can be a source of objective information for individual training.

Feedback

Most candidates for jobs are receptive to and appreciate performance feedback. Holding assessment centres gives you something to talk about. You can tell candidates what they did well on and what areas of weakness they need to improve.

Summing up

A well-developed and well-administered assessment centre can greatly improve a selection or promotional process. This is because we start from looking at the characteristics we require rather than concentrating on the technical competencies that enable the candidate to do the job at a basic level. The job of leading a team of subject experts, for example, is changing. Therefore you have to select people on the basis of the job that you want done and that is congruent with the aims of your organisation.

Action points

- Use the opportunity that recruitment brings to evaluate the strengths of your organisation.
- Determine the characteristics you require of the post holder.
- Use a range of assessment processes – an assessment centre – to evaluate the candidates' suitability.
- Use in-tray exercises, role plays, leaderless discussions, presentations and coaching sessions to gather evidence about each candidate's performance.
- Use the interview situation to explore the issues raised from the evidence collection.
- Develop scenarios as a means of asking candidates for their responses.
- Use the data to inform and give feedback.
- Give feedback to the successful candidate as well as the unsuccessful ones.

References and suggestions for further reading

Born M. and Jansen P. (1997) 'Selection and Assessment During Organisational Turnaround' in Herriot P. and Anderson N. (eds) *International Handbook of Selection and Assessment* John Wiley, Chichester

Brighouse T. and Woods D. (1999) *How to Improve Your School* Routledge, London

Cavanagh R.F. and Dellar G.B. (1996) 'The Development of an Instrument for Investigating School Culture' Paper presented to the Annual Conference of the American Educational Research Association, New York

Covey S. (1991) *Principle Centred Leadership* Simon and Schuster, London

Handy C. (1991) *The Age of Unreason* Arrow, London

Hargreaves A. (1994) 'Development and Desire: A Post-Modern Perspective' Paper presented to the Annual Conference of the American Educational Research Association, New Orleans

Kline P. (1993) *The Handbook of Psychological Testing* Routledge, London

Prahald C. and Hamel G. in Herriot P. and Anderson N. (eds) *International Handbook of Selection and Assessment* John Wiley, Chichester

Rees M. and Earles J. in Herriot P. and Anderson N. (eds) *International Handbook of Selection and Assessment* John Wiley, Chichester

Sternberg R. (1997) 'Tacit Knowledge and Job Success' in Herriot P. and Anderson N. (eds) *International Handbook of Selection and Assessment* John Wiley, Chichester

5   Is the honeymoon over?

Thursday, 15 March

Things to do today:

1   Prepare for the meeting with the head of Art.
2   Performance review for the head of PE.
3   Job description for second in Languages.
4   Evaluation of Year 8 parents' evening.
5   Evaluation of INSET session.
6   Prepare staff meeting presentation on assessment strategy.
7   End of term arrangements – talk about this.
8   Exam entry – see exams officer.
9   Performance indicators for PHSE?
10 Matinee performance of Cider with Rosie – contact primary schools.
11 Photocopy syllabus for Emma.
12 Meet Sarah.
13 Phone Teaching Personnel about cover for after Easter.

The first few months have been very nice – I've held a meeting with all my direct reports and I've spent a lot of time seeing how things are organised. It hasn't been possible simply to watch though – I've had to respond and get on and do things. Spoke to Julie yesterday – she said that in her first term she'd been able to spend a lot of time talking to people – because so many things are already in place there is less pressure to sort things out. I think that it will make things more difficult for her later on, though. Change management is always a challenge but the imperative for change is more obvious when there is a clear and identifiable need to do things differently.

I think that there is also an issue about being a sole deputy. I think that there is a different role for me as sole deputy compared to my colleagues who are one of two or even three people in the same position.

One of the things that I have been thinking about a great deal – and this stems from my own experience as a subject leader – is what the role of the middle manager is and how it is likely to change over time. What do I expect these people to do? It's relatively straightforward if all we expect is for books to be ordered and so on – but the issues of performance management will sharpen the focus that is required for these people.

On my list of things to consider is the staff meeting next week. I've thought a great deal about assessment. We need to make sure that we use all the data we collect on students in a consistent way. We need to make them accessible to people and present them in such a manner that they really inform planning. It's too easy to produce a set of tables with loads of figures that are completely meaningless and irrelevant. They have to make a difference and be seen to do so. Otherwise people will ignore the data and get fed up with being asked for assessment information.

Earlier in the book I argued that it was important for you as an aspirant deputy headteacher to have considered what sort of leader you wish to be. This chapter is called 'Is the honeymoon over?' because most new deputies find their first few weeks very pleasant in many respects. They are enjoyable because you are filled with the initial enthusiasm for the new job. You are anxious to please, to do your best and to be successful. In my case, I wanted the faith and trust that had been put in me by the head and governors to be justified by my work.

The first few weeks can be a source of considerable stress, owing to the challenge of getting to know the staff, becoming used to the school, and indeed coming to terms with the feeling of being constantly on duty. There is a shared feeling among deputies that you are on duty from the moment your car pulls up in the car park. There is no such thing as a private time; most deputies work with their door wide open. Indeed this is often expected. The only time that the door closes is when you are in a meeting with someone.

It is important to recognise the pressure that can build up in consequence.

However, the first few weeks are very nice for all that. You are doing the job you really wanted; you are an important person in the organisation. Depending on the type of school you work in and the time of year you are appointed, the first few days may be a maelstrom of activity, and some feelings of lack of control may characterise the early weeks. Staff will, in the main, excuse you for not knowing the history of events and, it is to be hoped, forgive you for the errors that ensue. But there comes a time when the real work has to begin.

The analogy that might be made is with visiting someone's house. For most of us, when we visit someone in his or her house, we observe their rituals, we respect their space, and the niceties of social interaction prevail. If we move in, however, the dynamic alters. To start with, the same relationship continues: you are in a kind of limbo, moving from guest to co-habitee. At first, you don't know what it means to be part of the household; you don't appreciate the way that people live together or what makes them function. This process of getting to know people is essential to the role.

This chapter is about learning to live in the house that is school. It is about developing a role in the school, how the new relationships are defined, and the challenges that arise when you consider your role in relation to the headteacher, the senior team, middle managers, the whole staff and the governors.

As deputy head, one of your most important relationships is with the headteacher. If you join a team as second or third deputy, then your relationships tend to be located in the hierarchy. For example, if you are responsible for pupil behaviour, then the relationship will be defined by the way in which you manage the behaviour and the leadership of, perhaps, heads of year and key stages.

The first section in this chapter considers your relationships with the head and senior team as a sole deputy.

The power of one: the case for the sole deputy

Missing from much of the discussion on the efficacy of school leadership is the role of the deputy head. Indeed, until recently, deputy heads were considered to be, at best, about to become extinct and, at worst, superfluous to the new leadership models. All the research on change and managing change (for example, Fullan and Stiegelbauer 1991) suggests that organisational change cannot happen overnight, that it cannot be mandated from the top without the endorsement and commitment of others throughout the organisation. Starratt (1999) argues, further, that change must proceed in an orderly fashion that entails dialogical exploration of assumptions, building trust and listening abilities, and addressing cultural as well as structural issues.

Much attention has been placed on the role of the headteacher, and the NPQH is testament to the qualities required for sustained school development and organisational improvement. However, against this background, in this section I want to argue the case for the deputy head and articulate why the role of the sole deputy head is one of the most exciting and professionally challenging posts in education.

To be sole deputy head in a large comprehensive school is to be in a unique position, and this section seeks to explore what makes this role distinctive. Some of the reasons are (not in any particular order):

- the nature of the relationship with the headteacher
- the function of the deputy head in relation to quality control
- the role of the sole deputy within a Senior Management Team
- the executive authority that comes from the position

In this section I argue that a relationship of both interdependence and dependence makes the role of sole deputy head unique to education. Gronn (1999) analyses the evolving delegated authority relationship between a headteacher and his or her deputy and, in so doing, highlights the importance of a neglected substitute for the direct exercise of leadership, namely the leadership duo or couple.

Couples typically comprise a partnership between the incumbents of a superordinate and a subordinate managerial role (Krantz 1989), the kind of mutually supportive dual relationship formed by a focal leader and a sympathetic key figure.

The nature of the relationship with the headteacher

The National Standards for Headteachers set out clearly the core purpose of headship: 'to provide professional leadership for a school that secures its success and improvement, ensuring high quality education for all its pupils and improved standards of learning and achievement'. This is a huge responsibility and there are a number of key phrases in the statement. The emphasis is on leadership, the outcomes of which are success and improvement. The headteacher has to ensure 'high quality education'. In addition, the headteacher is responsible for creating a productive, disciplined learning environment and for the day-to-day management, organisation and administration of the school. This chapter does not seek to set out headship as anything other than the greatest and ultimate challenge in education. The qualities required to create, develop and sustain a learning enterprise are immense, but this is, ultimately, the acid test of a headteacher's effectiveness. The role of the headteacher is diverse, areas of responsibility ranging from premises, to staff welfare, to exclusions to finance among many other things. I would argue that creating and sustaining a learning environment is better served by a broader base. It is imperative that leadership is sustained across the school. The nature of headship is so diverse, so wide-reaching and overarching that there is an absolute necessity for another person who, to all intents and purposes, is an *associate* head.

Implicit in the relationship between the head and sole deputy is the power bond; the head is the leader, the chief executive, the final word. However, a quality relationship in which the head and deputy work in partnership gives immense benefits. Krantz (1989) pointed to a paradox at the heart of the couple, namely 'each [individual] must trust the other whilst coping with the feelings of dependence on the other'.

How can this relationship be developed and sustained? Precisely because of the 'soleness': it is difficult for an intensely close relationship to be sustained over a long period of time with a large group. The difficulty of getting people to meetings in a busy school precludes this. Also, the quality of discussion between two leaders can be enhanced because their concentration is confined to one another. The closeness of this professional relationship should be characterised by empathy, sensitivity, candour and trust. As sole deputy, you are in a unique position because you can see the decision-making process. You can see how the head responds to events and situations, and will be able to support the head fully. However, there needs to be mutual sensitivity and this can only be achieved through a desire to achieve a genuine partnership. Gronn (1999) argues further that wedded to an implicitly understood world view or framework of values, and with each partner in the couple knowing the mind of the other, both the senior of the two (as the founder and framer of the new vision) and the junior (as the keeper or guardian of his or her mandate) build a joint and evolving understanding in their separate spheres and bailiwicks as the enterprise to whose realisation they are jointly committed is given shape.

The opportunities for partnership thinking are enhanced by this duality. For example, when creating a policy, there is opportunity for both philosophy and practice to align. My headteacher and I have spent many hours discussing how to move our school forward. On one occasion, we started a discussion on school development – four hours later we finished. This discussion visited philosophy, policy, politics and personal experience. The outcome was an alignment of purpose, the inspiration for a development plan which will shape our school for the next three years. But was this necessary? We have a plan, which reflects our desires and our beliefs – we own our plan. Consequently, we were able to facilitate a whole range of discussions with our staff. We sold it because it was ours and we believed in it. The intensity of this relationship emerges from a shared need and a mutual dependence. When the head is out of school, I am in charge. When he is in meetings, he relies on me to do his 'management by wandering about'. Our beliefs and our visions have aligned because of the time we have spent working together. Gronn (1999) asks the question: why do leadership couples gel? He concludes that there are four additional factors which make for a productive bonding: a rehearsed working relationship; a moral unity in which it is contained; sufficient space for each partner to exercise personal responsibilities; and a balance between their temperaments.

This kind of relationship is in many ways unique in schools. What characterises much of a teacher's professional life is the time spent alone – if being with thirty children counts as being alone – that is, without adult company. Teachers who undertake team teaching and work alongside one another quickly develop deep professional relationships that enable them to share and collaborate. However, for a school to be led by two people who have that commitment to one another in their professional lives makes for a powerful force.

The function of the deputy head in relation to quality control

As sole deputy head you are in a unique position in relation to the quality of teaching and learning; this is, in many ways, the most challenging aspect of the job. While the head has the responsibility for quality *assurance*, your role is that of quality *control*. Such a distinction is a necessary condition for effective school improvement. The headteacher needs to be able to represent the school and give account of the work that is done to the governors, OfSTED, parents, the community, etc. The functional aspect of this cannot become confused with the accountability and responsibility explicit in this relationship. As the arbiter of quality provision, the headteacher is served best by a functionary who is able to broker improvements in the quality of teaching and learning because of her immersion in the curriculum. The headteacher, as the chief executive of the school (Hughes 1988), has to take the overview of the work of the school. The deputy head is positioned to act as functionary.

Further, the nature of the relationship creates executive authority; this is a necessary condition for sustained improvement in the quality of teaching and learning. In this sense, the deputy head, because of the associate nature of the role, is placed to be the leading professional who can facilitate staff development and act as the role model for staff.

The executive authority that comes from the position and the preparation for headship

Being a sole deputy is an excellent preparation for headship. It provides you with the opportunity to lead the school. As I said before, when the head is away, I am it. This is not always that much fun because if things have gone wrong, there is a sense of isolation. However, many serving headteachers would, perhaps, say this is essential preparation for the next step. Being a sole deputy means you take on the full range of responsibilities and you are, of necessity, involved in every aspect of the school's work. Because of the proximity to the head and, indeed, the teaching role that deputies still have, you are in a unique position to lead. The sole deputy is immersed in the curriculum but needs to develop the ability to be a reflective practitioner. From this reflection emerge strategic thought and the executive authority to respond.

The NPQH needs to be seen in this context. It is important to see the qualification as being *for* headship not *of* headship. Being sole deputy forces you to reflect on the nature of school life and the dynamics of organisational change. The power base of associate headship enables a sole deputy to be proactive and dynamic. Being a sole deputy is a great opportunity if you want to lead. Immense opportunities proceed from the close relationship I have articulated. I am a leader in my own right. The creativity I am able to bring to my job results from the partnership mode in which I operate. The coherence this brings to the leadership of our school cannot be overstated; it is dynamic, charismatic and permeates the culture. We are required to transact our relations across an authority boundary and the head is held accountable for his own and my work performance. These two features constitute the source of our dependence on one another. Provided we manifest the additional properties of specialisation, differentiation and complementarity then, suggest Hodgson *et al.* (quoted in Gronn

1999), we will form an integrated and effective work unit. If this is not the case, then the relationship won't and perhaps can't work. The only logical solution then is for someone to go. Under such circumstances, it is likely that the deputy will go anyway, but for positive reasons based upon the search for success as a sole deputy. Promotion to headship may then result much quicker than would otherwise be the case.

The role of the sole deputy within a Senior Management Team

Headteachers usually know what they want – or at least can say what they want. A sensitive deputy head can, in time, recognise those things that are fixed and 'not open to discussion' and those where 'one is minded to take note of your views'. This places the sole deputy in a unique position as a facilitator in a Senior Management Team. The proximity of the role enables the deputy to say things that the head might find difficult or that might imply compromise. The headteacher's expectations of and for the SMT are not always easy to articulate; there is the difficulty inherent in making personal comments or directing remarks to people on whom so much responsibility is placed. However, because of the indirect power relationship (the hierarchical structure may tacitly allude to this), the deputy can be both part of the team and distant from it. An important dimension of my work is to create a sense of leadership within each curriculum area and to create the leadership couple relationship with each subject leader. In this way the whole process of building a school team will be based on qualitative relationships and a task culture.

One of the ways in which the work of a deputy headteacher differs from that of, say, a head of subject, is the proximity of relationships that develop within the Senior Management Team. However, the relationships are subjected to such a variety of influences that this particular aspect of the role demands further analysis.

The recent change in the structure of management teams has produced a new dynamic in many schools. Indeed, the names used to describe these groups vary considerably. In some schools they are called Senior Management Team (abbreviated to SMT, which has caused me some difficulty, as these are my initials), others refer to them as the School Leadership Team, the Central Management Team or some other such name. Just as the name varies, the composition varies too. In some schools, the group comprises the head and deputies; or it may be enlarged to include other senior staff (now called assistant heads instead of senior teachers). The function of the group is one of management and leadership, and the model used makes a statement about the leadership paradigm in operation.

Leadership is a sophisticated concept with as many different definitions as people who have attempted to make them. Leigh (1988) suggested a number of different ways of looking at leadership:

- a focus on group processes
- personality and its effects
- the art of inducing compliance
- an exercise in influence
- act or behaviour
- a form of persuasion
- power relationship
- an instrument of goal achievement
- a way of defining an individual's goal

Macbeath and Myers (1999) ask some similar questions. In evaluating leadership through school organisation and ethos, the following questions are suggested:

- Where does the school get its energy?
- Is there a sense of purpose and direction?
- From where and from whom does that sense come?
- How are decisions made?
- Where are the networks?
- What are the shared norms?
- How do norms change over time?

Defining the work of a leadership group as being the focus of group processes provides a useful concept here. The business of running a school (put in functional terms) is about making sure that the core activities occur; this includes scheduling classes on a timetable, arranging cover for absent staff, premises management, assessment arrangements, event management, student management, personnel management, etc. That the word 'management' has been used to define each of these tasks is deliberate; at a functional level, these activities are about managing a process. They are about establishing a system that starts with core requirements (i.e. children and teachers need to have somewhere to go and some purpose defined in the course of a day, so we organise them into classes, make decisions about what they should do during the day and arrange for teachers to deliver according to these purposes). At its most fundamental level, a school has this functional requirement; without that scheduling, it is in chaos. This example is provided to illustrate the principle of a systems model. A systems model of school management is a response to growing size and complexity. As managers, we seek to organise and process. We accept the notion that without management there is chaos, without organisation there is no process, without process there is no system. But implicit in this notion of organisational process is that to handle change you have to understand the whole and then sort out how the bits fit together. Indeed the words which characterise this approach are those used in the computer industry – input, outputs and the various processes in between. However, this systems model has a great impact on the way managers see change: if their premise is that the organisation is managed by constructing a process to address a rational need, then it can only change through its processes and systems. The complexity of organisational change, of which a school is a particular example, means that trying to create an interdependent organisation with tightly linked systems is beyond the scope of most, if not all, managers.

One analysis that follows this premise is that running a school (for want of a less contentious phrase) requires a number of people to direct the fundamental processes. The question arises, therefore, of whether the increase in the size of the leadership or management team signifies an acceptance of the broad nature of the assignments or whether it constitutes a further increase in the range of processes to be managed. In a sense it is both; for those who have been in education for more than, say, five years, the rate of growth of the management task has been considerable. Add to this the pressure for improvement and a target-driven achievement culture, and the need for a new approach to the running of our schools emerges.

Personality factors have been brought to the fore. School leadership is now seen as a dynamic and creative process; it is no longer confined to a model of change that starts with auditing, establishes the goal, sets out the process and manages it to achieve the goal. Crucially, there is no longer only one goal.

The newer models of management accept change and turbulence; despite this observation, the entire system is still bound together by shared values, sentiments and symbols. The manager is still concerned with interdependencies, but between different systems of action, not people. The emphasis has shifted from the group to the individual.

Working with governors

For many deputies, the relationship with the governors will be a new one. The role of governors in schools varies considerably and in many cases teachers have little contact with them. However, when you become a deputy the picture changes a good deal. As deputy head, you will often attend full governors' meetings and act as adviser to one committee or more. This is a very important part of the job because of the function of the governing body. Although the relationship between the governing body and the school will be determined through the headteacher, you will need to have a view on how they see this working out. For the most part, you and the head will provide the governors with information about the school and give a steer on the best courses of action. This means that documents have to be prepared in such a way that the necessary information is provided (bearing in mind that some of the governors will not be fully cognisant with educational matters) and the choices are set out in a way that allows governors to make an informed decision.

> For me, leadership means having a clear personal vision of what I want to achieve. I am committed to a set of values and principles. But I have to be in the thick of things, I have to work alongside my colleagues, sharing the power and developing the leadership of others.

The role of the middle manager

In this context the role of the middle manager, the head of department or subject leader has come to the fore. If the recent debate over performance management has achieved nothing else, it has reopened the issue of the expectations of the team leader. The image of the subject leader, head of department, director of . . . – whatever the particular choice of title – has for a long time been rooted in the notion of being the first among equals. What this section seeks to do is unpack this notion and contrast it with various models of school management. Further, I argue that a new model for middle management is required which embraces the needs of schools in the current age and for the future.

For those who have been in teaching for more than a decade, the notion of the subject leader is a recent one. Before, it was the head of department; when I was a probationer, this was the best mathematician. He could do those questions that others struggled with. If Mathematics teachers were unable to see their way through a problem, they always thought: 'Peter will know.' In Modern Languages, the head of department could speak more languages and knew more vocabulary than the other teachers in the department. For all subjects, there was an equivalent person who had the title, the accolades and expectations. However, the minimum requirement for subject knowledge in the 1990s was that teachers had an understanding and knowledge of the National Curriculum. Effective teaching requires a good deal more than that. Primary teachers need a thorough grasp of subjects across the key stages if progress and continuity are to be handled appropriately. Secondary teachers need to know where their subject fits into or alongside other subject areas.

MacGilchrist *et al.* (1997) argue, in this context, that the challenge for the 'Intelligent school' is to achieve a balance between shallow and deep learning. It is also to ensure balance across the curriculum. Effective teaching is characterised by the teacher's ability to construct learning experiences in a way that builds on pupils' prior knowledge both in particular subjects and across the curriculum. MacGilchrist *et al.* suggest further that much more could and should be done to organise subject planning around key themes, skills and concepts; this will reduce the sense of overload that the National Curriculum can give and encourage greater understanding by pupils, as well as enabling them to relate more systematically to their prior learning.

The function of subject knowledge is not the main topic of this debate. However, the need for subject planning around key themes, skills and concepts requires a different kind of leadership from the one that has pervaded many curriculum departments. It is more discursive; it is a creative dynamic process that demands a different model of leadership and management in our schools.

The head of department – what has happened to this person? Why was this acknowledged expert found wanting? Because expertise in a subject did not equate with management skill and leadership attributes. As expectations were raised about the outcomes of the education system – the need for results and raised standards – then there needed to be a transition from this notion of the subject expert to one who could manage a group of teachers and take responsibility for the results.

The obstacles to collegiality are immense. Historically, the relationships between teachers may have been seen as the major obstacle to change, whereas their working conditions were not given much attention. Lodge (1988), in his novel Nice Work, describes a scene where the department is discussing its future.

> *But collegiality – that is a core value. But what does this mean in this context? Nice Work by David Lodge illustrates the need for some pragmatism in this respect.*

Like everything else in the Department, the Agenda Committee had a history, and a folklore, which Robyn had gradually pieced together from various sources. For decades the Head of Department had been a notorious eccentric . . . his successor, Dalton, was obliged by a new University statute to hold regular Department Committee meetings, but had cunningly defeated the democratic intention behind this rule by keeping the agenda of such meetings a secret unto himself . . . To counter this strategy, Philip Swallow, then a Senior Lecturer freshly energised by his exchange visit to America, had managed to secure the establishment of a new sub-committee called the Agenda Committee whose function was to prepare business for discussion by the full Department Committee. Swallow had inherited this apparatus . . . and used it . . . to consider the Department's policy on any given issue, and how it might be presented to the full Department Committee with the minimum risk of contentious debate.

At its meeting the department realised that as a result of its attempt to preserve everyone's interests and wishes it would have to set 173 separate Finals papers. This gives an amusing illustration of the muddle that can ensue when the collegial model is taken at face value. It has not yet been realised that the implication of adopting a collegial model is precisely that – a muddle. Too often, middle managers have felt caught in the bind of having to satisfy the demands made by the school leadership team and being unwilling or unable (for a variety of reasons) to accommodate the needs of the change in role. Often, managers have regarded their colleagues as friend first and subordinate second. Confusion has ensued; some have felt unable or unwilling to challenge practice, some have existed in denial.

Perhaps we have tried to preserve both collegiality and professionalism, and failed to appreciate what this means. For many, there has been a sense of 'role conflict'; some who had seen themselves as the 'first among equals' are now being required to act as line managers. Others have cultivated friendships as a management strategy – in the absence of any other. Some have seen their role as an administrative one – ordering books, placing children in sets, writing exam papers, deciding on exam syllabi: purely functional tasks which ignore the responsibility for quality control and associated monitoring processes. The consequence of these actions has been a conflict of what people can, will, want to and are obliged to do. Even when faced with some extreme examples of incapability, some subject leaders are unwilling to challenge poor teaching because they feel that their personal relationships will be affected and they don't want that. Who does? Who wants to have those difficult conversations that may lead to a long-time colleague being disciplined? But this is the job. School leaders have to acknowledge this difficulty in their management of subject leaders and understand the 'role conflict' that some will experience. Hargreaves (1972) identified eight sources of 'role conflict':

1. Where an actor simultaneously occupies two positions whose roles are incompatible [*i.e. wanting to preserve a friendship after it has become untenable*]
2. Where there is a lack of consensus amongst the occupants of a position about the content of a role [*i.e. when the post holder is in denial about the expectations of the role*]
3. Where there is a lack of consensus amongst the occupants of one of the complementary role positions [*i.e. when the members of the team refuse to accept the role the subject leader is playing*]
4. Where an actor's conception of his role conflicts with the expectations of a role partner [*i.e. when the subject leader's view is at variance with the teacher's*]
5. Where role partners have conflicting expectations [*i.e.*

where the subject leader and teacher disagree about the remit of the subject leader]

6. Where a single role partner has incompatible expectations [*i.e. where the teacher expects the team leader to solve their problems*]

7. Where role expectations are unclear [*i.e. where responsibility is denied*]

8. Where an actor lacks basic qualities required for adequate role performance [*i.e. the subject leader does not have the skills or profile to carry out the task*].

Since Hargreaves was writing from a interactive perspective the notion of role conflict was bound to play a significant part in his account of interpersonal relationships. However, from a functionalist perspective, the concept of role is based on an 'ideal type' and the national standards for subject leaders perhaps offer a good example of this principle. In practice, variation always exists in how people play the roles they are allotted.

This is change – it is change to the way in which people have worked together (or not as the case may be). An important part for me to play is to make this happen in practice. This will affect the way in which I organise meetings with people and my methods of monitoring their work. Moreover, as we sustain the school team then the values have to be consistent over time.

What does this all mean for those charged with leading schools? Those in middle management (subject leaders, co-ordinators, etc.) need to recognise the changing nature of leadership. We need a definition of teamwork that will be sustainable in the current context. This means thinking about relationships in new ways. West and Allen (1997) introduce the concept of a 'Work Team'; this is characterised as follows:

1   Team members have shared objectives in relation to their work.
2   Team members interact with each other in order to achieve those shared objectives.
3   Team members have more or less well-defined roles, some of which are differentiated.
4   Teams have organisational identity; that is, they have a defined organisational function and see themselves as a group within a larger organisation.
5   Teams are not large enough to be defined as an organisation.

The role of the team leader is crucial. It is about ensuring that there is sufficient clarity on the nature of the role and the function of the team. Before personnel are selected for a particular team, attention needs to be given to the design or structure of the work that the team members will do and the roles they will occupy. Typically, teachers are recruited and selected to work as part of a group because they appear to have the particular set of technical skills and experience deemed necessary for particular aspects of the job. This is, of course, entirely reasonable. Also reasonable, however, would be an examination of the degree to which candidates have the personal characteristics necessary to work effectively as part of the team.

But how should the demands of team leadership be affected by the remit of the team leader? All those working in schools are constantly engaged in change; there is no steady state. The continual drive to raise standards, the perpetual debate on how things could be done better, the imperative to add value mean that, to an extent, all managers are 'turnaround managers'. Considering the expectations and the task focus of the team as a whole makes the leadership model clearer. By considering the functional and interpersonal aspects at the group level of analysis, several studies suggest facilitative effects of heterogeneity; the perpetual change that characterises the new steady state requires different inputs for collaborative effect. This pattern is most likely when the attributes in question are skills or educational specialisation and the dependent variable is team performance. The demands for organisational turnaround that have characterised the last decade have produced a number of trends in schools: internationalisation and globalisation of educational theory and practice, mergers, societal changes in the competency profile of applicants for teaching, active organisational policies to address a permanently changing environment, and governmental influence.

Born and Jansen (1997) describe the contemporary manager as the 'turnaround manager'. They argue that the challenge lies in dealing with the reinterpretation of reality. Transformational leadership is suggested as an effective way of leading turnaround. Awareness, persuasiveness, an internal locus of control and prudent risk taking, among other things, have been found to be important personality factors for leaders of organisational change. The domain of the middle manager cannot be solely located in a bureaucratic model; the National Standards for Subject Leaders tried to profile the role of the subject leader (Teacher Training Agency 1998). However, the collegial structure of many subject groups (or indeed other groups) is flawed by their neglect of the responsibility for raising standards and, often, the reluctance of these key professionals to grasp the nettle which means telling their closest professional co-workers that they have to change. For middle managers to be able to do this, the myth of collegiality needs to be quashed. To assert a collegial model in this climate is flawed. The leadership and management needs of schools mean that to attempt to operate collegially results at best in role conflict and at worst in pseudo-collegiality. The demand is for quality. Handy (1995) writes that quality is not easy to achieve. It needs the right equipment, the right people and the right environment. The effective organisation, today, is learning fast to come to terms with the new people it needs and the new culture of consent. To assert that teachers can merely be commanded, however, is to miss the point. Often there is no one to command them. We will all be judged increasingly by our results rather than by our methods. Authority will devolve not on those best able to do the job themselves but on those best able to help others do the job better, by developing their skills, by liaising with the rest of the organisation, by organising the work more efficiently, by helping them to make the most of resources and by continual encouragement and example.

There was a time when schools had a curriculum deputy and a pastoral deputy (and some still do). Lots of things have happened to these roles: the downsizing of the hierarchical structure (paradoxically being replaced by an enlarged structure some years later) created a model with one deputy headteacher plus a group of senior teachers. Some schools held the enlightened view that there was no curriculum/pastoral divide and to create one through the organisational structure was at best unnecessary and at worst destructive of collective responsibility. To suggest that the job of a curriculum leader can be stated in terms of what is taught and how it is assessed shows a gap in basic understanding of the ways in which human organisations work. Learning is not just about objectives, school bells and assessment models; it is about the ways in which people interact and the creation of a learning culture.

However, the enormity of the task of managing an ever-changing curriculum requires both creativity and tenacity of approach. The sheer size of the modern school curriculum means that any change has to occur through the empowerment of subject leaders and the development of their skills. In this respect, the job of the curriculum manager or curriculum leader has become considerably more complex. Even the best plans for innovation and progression are only as valuable as their results. A system is needed, requiring a discursive co-operative manner that is, in some respects, counter to the traditional deputy headteacher role.

As deputy headteacher, you have to work in areas of which you have little knowledge. For some post holders, the last time they looked at a Geography book may have been when they were at key stage 3 (or its equivalent). Yet, as deputy headteacher, you have to be able to discuss the Geography curriculum with the subject leader. Most challengingly, you may have to work with the leader of a subject of which you have no knowledge at all. This is particularly the case in Modern Languages and in some relatively recent additions to the school curriculum such as Politics, Psychology and Sports Studies. The point is that your work with subject leaders is not about the subject. You may not know Russian, but you know about learning. You may not be able to advise the head of Sports Studies about the best way to teach the anatomy section, but you do know how to measure the efficacy of any assessment model developed in response to certain objectives.

There are a number of ways in which, as deputy headteacher, you can address the issues confronting you and create a modus operandi that works and enables you to keep track of all that you are required to do. Getting to know the subject leaders is critical to the success that you will achieve. However, you have to move from knowing about a subject in general to knowing about its particular situation in your school. To do this in a challenging and yet supportive way is a tightrope that you have to learn to walk. To move the school forward, there has to be a healthy debate and you can only take part in this from a position of in-depth knowledge.

Regular meetings

These are essential to developing effective working relationships with the curriculum leaders. One way of establishing these relationships is to set up the initial meetings with a defined agenda. At the inaugural meeting the topics for discussion might be as follows:

- GCSE and A Level pass rates over the past three years
- staffing changes
- curriculum changes
- targets for the coming year
- developments in the subject nationally and locally

There may be other topics to add, but the advantage of such an agenda is that it establishes that the initial focus of the meeting is the subject and the results. However, the discussion will move on to the staff in the department. Further discussion of targets for the next year and development planning can help to create the agenda for the next meeting.

When I set up my first meetings with heads of subject, I gave them a pro forma with a number of questions relating to the topics listed above. Included in the pro forma was a section entitled 'is there anything you would like to discuss?' I also suggested a meeting date and time. I asked them to let me have a copy of their completed pro forma the day before the meeting. The advantage of this approach was to enable both parties to prepare for the meeting. I don't know if any of the subject leaders were nervous about this meeting; at the very least, I was an unknown quantity. But the agenda was clear. People knew what I wanted to talk about. Some colleagues might have asked people to tell them some or all this information as part of the meeting. My approach was different; if you are asking people to spend a period of time with you, it is important for the meeting to be focused on the issues, not on fact finding. Including the section on 'Any other business' enabled me to anticipate any difficulties and assess the potential for the meeting.

The results of these first meetings varied a good deal in accordance with people's confidence in talking about their subject. Three outcomes, however, were consistent:

1   I had a profile of each subject area – its successes, the staffing issues, the curriculum issues and its potential for the future – at that point.
2   The agenda for the next meeting – by thinking through the material that the subject leaders had provided and the answers to the questions I posed, it was possible to construct an agenda around the task set.
3   The date and time of the next meeting.

A feature of my work with subject leaders has been the records I keep of each meeting. Some deputy headteachers keep an exercise book where they record the main points of each meeting. I write notes from each meeting and provide a copy for the headteacher and the subject leader. This is an example of a meeting report with the head of Art.

Cheryl

At our meeting we discussed the following:

- The assessment model you developed last term is being implemented this year – this will enable students to record their progress over time.
- Sarah is preparing a unit of work for Year 8. She has made a very good start and you are delighted with her work. She will clearly need to be supported as she progresses through the year, but the prospects are excellent.
- The Year 9 sow [scheme of work] is still to be done. You have changed the format of the sow following our discussions and you will supply me with copies, for my records. Thank you.
- Developing the Art curriculum – there are other courses that we could explore and these include Ceramics, Graphic Design, Textiles and Art and Design (GNVQ). The CPG [Curriculum Planning Group] would be interested in pursuing these courses and we agreed to discuss this further at our next meeting. You are going to research these possibilities in anticipation of that meeting.
- Premises – you have some concerns about the cleaning of your room – if these concerns are realised, please see LJW in the first instance. There is also an issue about accommodation – this is an on-going matter, exacerbated by the large number of people wanting to do Art. This is a very good thing, but will need to be considered fully.

Our next meeting is on Thursday, 2 May, 2.15–2.45pm

ST

This system works for me because it enables me to keep records in a manageable way. The report is filed on my computer. I email the report to the headteacher and the subject leader (if possible, as not everyone is on the network). This approach suits my style and it shows subject leaders that the meeting they have had with me is important enough for me to provide a record of it. It is easy in a busy week (and this approach does demand considerable time) to forget what has been discussed and agreed. This approach makes it all public. It also means that the headteacher is fully appraised of the work that is being done. It also means that an on-going dialogue is established and sustained over time. This will enable you to challenge views over time.

An important point to note, however, is that you cannot solve all the problems at once. You cannot tackle every single issue in the first week; the job is not the sprint. A moment's reflection will testify to the veracity of this observation, but a demanding headteacher can make you feel that immediately isn't quick enough. However, it is important to take the long-term view. There may be occasions when you have to give way, but if you steer your course consistently, then opportunities arise for you to put your point of view.

Planning staff meetings

An important dimension to the team approach is those occasions when the whole staff meet together. In Chapter 3, I described the staff briefing. Here, I discuss planned staff meetings where a particular issue is being raised.

In a large organisation, the occasions when the whole staff come together can be infrequent and it is therefore vital that such meetings are considered carefully. A meeting has to represent the best practice. If a core value of the leadership team is punctuality, then the meeting has to start on time. If a core principle is that meetings should have a published agenda, be effectively chaired and so on, then any meeting led by the leadership group needs to be conducted with this in mind.

Moreover, if the values of the leadership team are based on shared decision-making, then meetings can't be occasions when staff are dictated to. There may be a case for some transmission of information (for example, explaining the budget) but where philosophical or pedagogical models are being articulated, the whole staff need to be engaged.

Leadership has to be about creating a climate in which change is seen as challenging and professionally invigorating. The staff forum is therefore an important one. Preparing to present to such a group is a task that has to be considered.

Making presentations

There are a number of steps that are important when planning and delivering a presentation.

1 Decide what is the message that you want to get across. What do you want to say?
2 List the objectives of the presentation. Do you want to tell people about changes to coursework, the literacy strategy, etc.?
3 Determine your audience – staff, parents, students, governors, etc. This is important because you will need to consider how much information is already known by the audience.
4 How long will the presentation be? (If it is an hour-long meeting, 10–15 minutes might be enough.)
5 Who will be involved in making the presentation? (Sometimes it is better to do these things on your own, other times working with a colleague is beneficial.)
6 Brainstorm the theme and then start to create the presentation. Deciding whether to use PowerPoint or a flipchart or a whiteboard or whatever is fundamental because it will determine the type of presentation you give. A PowerPoint presentation is suitable for a large group and enables you to concentrate on talking to people and getting a certain message across. A flipchart is suitable for a smaller group (say, up to fifteen) and allows you to be interactive, but prepare some of the sheets in advance). A whiteboard presentation can be very useful because the presentation builds up as you deliver.
7 Discuss your presentation with someone else. Decide what will happen when the presentation is over. Will there be activities to follow?

There are also practical issues to consider when preparing for a presentation:

1   Set up the presentation area: make sure the projector works, if using an OHP. Make sure that the screen is clean. In all cases make sure that everyone can see.

2   Organise the cables: it's easy to trip over cables when concentrating on the presentation.

3   Practise the presentation: the advantage of using a PowerPoint presentation is that you do not have to look at the screen and can operate the presentation via the mouse.

4   Do not be too ambitious. If you haven't done this sort of thing before, prepare thoroughly and ask for help.

The value of a presentation is that it gives you the opportunity to articulate your position and explain yourself. Allowing time for questions is an important part of this work and can be built into the structure.

Much of this is about communication. The benefits of this whole-staff approach are enormous: a real sense of shared enterprise can develop. The aims of the school must, of course, be consistent and coherent at all times, and it is particularly important to remember this when things go wrong. Things will go wrong because of the nature of school life and its dependence on relationships between individuals and groups. Having a view on the basis of all the relationships that make up the organisational culture goes some way to resolving these problems.

A deputy headteacher colleague, Tom, told me of a problem he had with one of his direct reports. Tom's job is to line manage the pastoral heads; he is thus responsible for behaviour management in the school. One of the heads of year was consistently and persistently undermining Tom, not just with students but with other staff. Tom had never had the right opportunity to tackle this with the head of year. Matters came to a head when Tom entered the staffroom to find a group of staff discussing what his response might be to a major disciplinary occurrence in which a child had been abusive to a teacher. The child had been the subject of protracted discussions between parents and the head of year. It had been agreed that in view of the child's circumstances, exclusion was not the right option. Tom later heard that this same head of year had been openly criticising his 'lack of action' and 'lack of support for the staff'. Tom asked me what I thought we should do and this is how it was resolved:

- Tom asked the head of year to come to his office the next day, and asked him if reports of what he had said in the staffroom had been correct. The head of year said 'yes'.
- Tom explained that what the head of year was proposing was contrary to the agreement already made. Tom asked the head of year if he still agreed with the proposed action.
- Tom stated how he felt about the head of year's management of the situation and the course of action was confirmed. Tom asked the head of year to let him know if he disagreed with any decision. He said he would do so.

By tackling the problem quietly, Tom was able to demonstrate a cool head and say what he wanted. I know it was difficult for him to do this; he was furious when he told me about it.

This incident illustrates some important lessons for the deputy headteacher:

- colleagues don't always represent the views of the deputy headteacher accurately
- it will happen to you: when you go into the staffroom it will fall quiet
- you may be very cross about something but you are the one who has to keep cool and tackle the problem
- the opportunity to resolve difficult issues will arise but you may have to wait

It is when these critical moments occur that you realise who you are and that you cannot be an ordinary member of the staff. These times can be quite difficult; it is not pleasant to go into a room and know that others are discussing you, perhaps in less than flattering terms. This is where strength of character and belief in yourself as a leader come to the fore. It is where the principles of your leadership style really matter. If you are consistent in your approach, if you treat all in the same way and chart your course in an open and honest manner, these attributes will see you through the difficult times.

Action points

- You need to have a vision of how to build a whole-school team. This means thinking about the role of the senior team, middle manager and so on.
- How does your role fit with the leadership group?
- What kind of leader do you want to be?
- Are you a leader or a manager?
- How do you reconcile the demands of the job with your principles?
- How to maintain your principles in the light of the new job
- How do you create a model that works for you and your school?
- How do you present your work to governors, staff, parents and students?
- Principle-centred leadership is a fundamental characteristic and will help to sustain you when things go wrong.

Leadership is a challenging concept and relies on reflection and the desire to make things work in the right way. Macbeath and Myers (1999) evaluate leadership by asking:

- Where does the school get its energy?
- Is there a sense of purpose and direction?
- From where and from whom does that sense come?

- How are decisions made?
- Where are the networks?
- What are the shared norms?
- How do norms change over time?

References and suggestions for further reading

Born M. and Jansen P. (1997) 'Selection and Assessment During Organisational Turnaround' in Herriot P. and Anderson N. (eds) *International Handbook of Selection and Assessment* John Wiley, Chichester

Fullan M. and Stiegelbauer S. (1991) *The New Meaning of Educational Change* 2nd edn Teachers College Press, New York

Gronn P. (1999) 'Leadership from a Distance: Institutionalizing Values and Forming Character at Timbertop, 1951–61' in Begley P.T. and Leonard P. (eds) *The Values of Educational Administration* RoutledgeFalmer, London

Handy C. (1995) *The Age of Unreason* Arrow, London

Hargreaves D. (1972) *Interpersonal Relations and Education* Routledge and Kegan Paul, London

Hughes M. (1988) 'Leadership in Professionally Staffed Organisations' in Glatter R. *et al.* (eds) *Understanding School Management* Open University Press, Milton Keynes

Krantz J. (1989) 'The Managerial Couple: Superior–Subordinate Relationships as a Unit of Analysis' *Human Resource Management*, **28**

Leigh A. (1988) *Effective Change: Twenty Ways to Make it Happen* The Institute of Personnel Management, London

Lodge D. (1988) *Nice Work* Penguin, London

Macbeath J. and Myers K. (1999) *Effective School Leaders* Pearson Education, London

MacGilchrist B., Myers K. and Reed J. (1997) *The Intelligent School* Paul Chapman, London

Noble T. and Pym B. (1970) 'Collegial Authority and the Receding Locus of Power' in Bush T. (ed.) *Managing Education: Theory and Practice* Open University Press, Buckingham

Starratt R. (1999) 'Moral Dimensions of Leadership' in Begley T. and Leonard P. (eds) in *The Values of Educational Administration* RoutledgeFalmer, London

Teacher Training Agency (1998) *National Standards for Headteachers* London

Tranter S. (2000) *From Teacher to Middle Manager – Making the Next Step* Pearson, London

Weber M. (1947) 'Legal Authority in a Bureaucracy' in Bush T. (ed.) *Managing Education: Theory and Practice* Open University Press, Milton Keynes

West M. and Allen 'Selecting for Teamwork' in Herriot P. and Anderson N. (1997) *International Handbook of Selection and Assessment* John Wiley, Chichester

6　If you are going to get better, you have to learn more

Friday, 15 June

As the school year has progressed the need for personal reflection on my practice has, if anything, become more important. I've always been someone who thinks deeply about her work; but in the maelstrom of school life – when there are so many things to do, it would be too easy to act first and think later.

I discussed this with Leo, a headteacher colleague. Leo has been head of his school for twelve years now and this is his second headship. We were talking about the need for reflection – and he gave me some very good advice. Leo said that he had seen a number of initiatives come and go over the years and that there was a real sense in which some things were coming full circle. He used the game of cricket as an analogy.

Cricket is a not a game that is characterised by speed. It is a game that is played over the course of several hours, even days. It depends on the efforts of each person in the team – from the opening batsperson to the 'night watch-man'. Without effective bowling and fielding the game is poor. Without judicious umpiring, the game collapses.

But cricket is not a game about rules – the umpire has to interpret and judge. A fast pace does not always mean an early victory. One star player will not produce a team victory.

When children enter our school they do so for some of their most important and life-shaping years. When teachers join the profession – for many this will be their life's work. It is easy to jump on bandwagons and to pursue the latest fad

— but the exercise of judgement, in deciding what is the best course, is something that requires maturity and reflection.

Moreover, it requires a deep understanding of how people function. We need to consider how to motivate others and how to sustain that enthusiasm that we see in newly qualified teachers.

As Leo said, 'Judgment is all'.

Anyone reading this book will want to be considered competent at his or her job. We want to be good at what we do and we want to be seen to be good at what we do. It is these two aspects of competence that require us all to evaluate our work and, indeed, plan for the future.

An aspect of the job of being a deputy head is the ephemeral nature of what is carried out each day combined with a long-term view that necessarily goes with it. A colleague in his first term as a deputy was telling me about the challenges that he had encountered. He was saying that he couldn't believe how much people varied in their approach to work. This was his example. Like all others in this role, he sends out memos to staff asking for information. It is good practice to include a deadline for the return. He said, 'I can't believe how many people just don't respond to my memos by the deadline and how much chasing up of these things I have to do!' Most people in a management role will know what this feels like. It's the same when we set homework for our students and they don't do it on time. The challenge for school managers here lies in how to make sure that deadlines are met and that the business of leading and managing a school does not collapse because of failure to deliver on time.

In Chapter 3, there is a description of the kind of deputy I wanted to be. I think all those who embark on this road want to be the best they can be. The tension lies surely in an acceptance of the frailties of the world in which we live and the frustration when things don't go to plan. It is dealing with this aspect of work, the search for competence, to which this chapter is devoted. The chapter is divided into four sections, not because the job can be segmented, but to provide a framework for us to consider the reflective skill that the work of a deputy demands.

Four main headings seem to arise in this context:

1 Professional knowledge

This is about knowing what it means to bring about change, both at an individual and an organisational level. Change management has been one of the most important features of life in schools over the past decade or so and there are few signs that it is in decline. However, fundamental to the change process is some understanding of how people are motivated and how your actions affect those around you. This is where the distinction between management and leadership models comes to the fore; the processes may be right, but the ways in which they are implemented will determine the outcomes. Change doesn't occur in a vacuum. The educational world is a market place where the product is bought and sold at a price; understanding the local, national and global market place is vital.

2 Basic role skills

It seems somewhat obvious to state that in order to bring about improvement you need to know what you are trying to improve. But we also need to know whether what we seek to improve is capable of improvement. The ability to analyse information and present it in a way that engages those around us is of increasing importance as the quantity and quality of data grow.

But the deputy head can never just be a person who produces graphs and tables of data. Without the ability to work with individuals and groups, to look forward and show the path, much of the analysis will be wasted. Working with teachers is very much about developing people. The prize of excellence has to be kept to the fore, but must be part of the value system of the organisation.

3 Core skills

Without organised management, schemes fall apart and so one of your essential functions as deputy head is information collection and promulgation. This has to be done in a co-ordinated manner, otherwise the 'big picture' gets lost in the detail (and, too often, in a mountain of paper). But being a deputy isn't about churning out paper. It is about generating ideas, planning and sequencing.

4 Characteristics

There are times when the job of being a deputy is very difficult (and I'm sure that all of us, whatever our occupation, could make the same remark about our jobs) but there is a need in a value-driven, people-centred organisation to place the building of relationships at the fore. But this demands a level of persistence and independence that enables us to see the world of our school as it is and know what needs to happen to make it as we want it to be.

The deputy head as a 'change agent'

A useful way of thinking about this matter is to consider a distinction between 'areas of competence' (i.e. aspects of the job which you must perform effectively) and 'competencies' (i.e. aspects of the job that enable you to develop particular areas of competence). There are a number of possibilities for this approach but in terms of your role as part of the leadership team in the school, I want to consider the deputy head as a 'change agent' in the context of this model.

The change agent has professional knowledge, basic role skills, core skills and characteristics. Taking each one in turn, we can consider what competencies the deputy head brings to the post and what needs to be developed in order to ensure that your career stays on track.

Firstly, the *professional knowledge* that is required for the role involves *knowing the change process*. The Industrial Society produced its own list of headteacher competencies (in MacBeath and Myers 1999) and three of these were about managing change: looking at possible future challenges, encouraging new ways of doing things and treating mistakes as learning opportunities. If the role of the headteacher is to look for these challenges, where does this leave the deputy head? I think that if one pursues the idea that only the headteacher can see the new ideas, then the organisation is in trouble; surely in a school with an intellectually able staff, the possibilities are endless. However, as deputy you have an important function to ensure that the staff's professional knowledge is sufficient to facilitate the change process. If there are times when there is insufficient information, then there has to be an element of judgement. If the facts are unknown, then is there a need for change to be initiated or for some planning to be left until the pattern is clearer. In terms of the deputy head's professional development, then, reading and discussing the articles in professional journals is clearly beneficial here. So, too, is being part of a network of like professionals. Initiatives such as 'Talking Heads' – the website for headteachers – may prove useful but often the network of contacts that are facilitated at local meetings can be the most instructive.

Reading the TES over the weekend is essential! At one level it informs me on how educational ideas are being developed across the world but also it expresses opinion and this is important for a sole deputy, in particular. There are a number of other journals – Managing Schools Today, Headlines and Croner – that are important too. It's about keeping up to date and being aware of ideas and what's going on.

Doing things in new ways is an everyday part of the deputy's lot; that is what makes the job exciting. However, in the first few months of the job, it is difficult to appreciate the virtue of doing things in new ways. One of the tasks that fall under my responsibility is the organisation of parents' evenings – those evenings where parents are invited to the school to discuss their children's progress. Another part of my job is to manage the assessment and reporting processes. Going to a new school and thinking about how to organise these important features of the school year present a range of choices.

Being given the job of leading these things is all very well. There is a purely operational component to the tasks. In relation to the parents' evenings these are:

- writing the letter to parents informing them about the evening (date, time, venue, etc.)
- arranging for appointment sheets to be given to staff and students so that appointments can be made
- seeing the caretaker to arrange for chairs and tables to be put out
- finding name plates for the tables
- organising tea for the staff
- clearing up

One of the important things to remember as a new deputy head is that these things have been done before. It is easy to fall into the trap of thinking, 'If I don't do it, then no one will'. However, it is

---

The first parents' evening I attended as deputy head was organised with all the tables in the assembly hall facing the same way. Parents stood in a long line. Apart from the noise, the evening looked confrontational. The next time we arranged the tables so that the hall was divided into two, with groups facing the centre. The effect was incredible. A small change made for a friendlier feel to the occasion. The point of this is to illustrate how the new deputy can bring new ways of doing things to a school — there is an operational part of the job — that is how things get done, but the job gives us the opportunity to think of things in new ways.

also very easy to presume things have been done and hence not check that this is the case. This is when mistakes and omissions happen. The point being made here is that all this is operational stuff. It is about making sure that things happen. If all that you do is make sure that the above are in place, then the job will have been done. But the opportunity for making a difference will have been lost.

The opportunity to make a difference can be taken in many ways. Reading the letter that is sent to parents, you may see a need for a rewrite. Instead of a letter that tells them when the evening is, a warmer, friendlier one that invites parents and emphasises the importance of the event may serve the purposes better. Add to this the opportunity for a mail-merge facility where a personal invitation from you (or the head of year or tutor) is written, and the possibilities grow. At a school where attendance at such events is poor, then allowing sufficient time for replies to be returned and phone calls to be made can raise attendance rates still further. Looking at the appointment sheet, fresh eyes can see new possi- bilities; for example, a perennial problem is that of appointments being made too close together (i.e. we wanted appointments to be at ten-minute intervals, but to last for only five minutes, thus allowing for 'travelling time'). By making the last appointment at ten minutes to the hour, we gained a five-minute 'catch up'. By issuing two different appointments sheets, one with times of, say, 4.05, 4.15, 4.25, and the other of 4.10, 4.20, 4.30, etc., the problem of making the appointments can be addressed. However, when you start to think about these things in new ways you create a whole range of issues to tackle. Once you open up the debate about such things as the venue, the seating, the letters home, etc., the function and purpose of these events come into sharper focus.

Moving on to the parents' evening itself:

- At what time of day should the event occur?
- Should it happen once a year and what opportunities are there for parents to meet subject teachers at other times? Are such opportunities required?
- How do teachers inform their colleagues so that the issues addressed at a previous event are not revisited?

- Is it an occasion for the teachers to inform the parents or for the parents to ask questions?
- How can it be ensured that parents are given good-quality information?
- What steps are in place to ensure that teachers can speak freely but not be subjected to harassment?
- Should students be invited and be part of the event?
- What is the role of the school leaders at such an event? Are they the hosts or is the head of year?
- What is the role of the tutor at such an event?

> These are important issues to consider and they illustrate the role that the deputy head has in bringing about organisational change. These questions also illustrate that in seeking to improve one aspect of the job, so many other things are called into question. The professional knowledge required for the job of deputy head is not just about knowledge of the change process but also about a management approach.

The big picture: parents' evenings and school reports

You need to see the whole picture: sending out reports just before parents' evenings may provide the opportunity to discuss the issues raised in them, but parents may think that there is no need to attend the evening, because they know from the report what the teacher thinks. Similarly, the teacher may not have anything new to say at the parents' evening, having just written a report. This is all fine if the purpose of the document is to obviate the need for the interview. But a school then misses an opportunity to engage in dialogue with parents about the progress of their child. In addition, if the report is poor, an opportunity to address the issues and engage the parents in supporting the child is valuable.

By separating the functions of school reports and parent's evenings, we expose the school to a debate with far-reaching implications, some of which are:

- What makes a quality report?
- Should reports be summative or formative?
- At what time of year should a report be written? If it is summative, then the end of the year is the most logical time for the majority of students (but think how difficult it would be for a teacher to write reports on all their students in July).
- If the report is formative, how long does the teacher need to assess the progress made and set targets? (This calls into issue the communication structures within departments. At the start of a year, do teachers know the learning targets for the students in their classes? Do Year 7 teachers know the targets of their primary colleagues?)
- Should the report itself be continuous, following on from the previous year? This would mean teachers have to comment on the targets set in the previous report and set new ones for the next period.
- To whom should a report be addressed? Is the report about the child or for the child? If the report is written about the child, then how do we engage him or her in the reporting process?
- What is the role of the subject leader, the tutor and the head of year in this process?
- What role should the school leaders play in this process?

Models of management and leadership and professional development

Learning about models of management and differing approaches to the task of leadership is an area that lends itself well to professional development. There are a lot of books which describe particular models (some of which are listed in this book) but only particularly reflective practitioners are able to analyse their own performance and consider it in the light of grounded theory. It is beneficial to engage in some kind of study programme, an MA or similar forum.

The value of this cannot be overestimated; by looking at management models and leadership styles and examining your own practice you learn the practice of reflection. It may be difficult to imagine finding the time to undertake study, but most courses do recognise the busy lives that we lead.

The approach taken by the Open University is a good example of this. Its courses are designed to meet teachers' needs by providing a supported distance study mode. The courses are practical in nature; an assignment might be 'Examine or undertake the process of planning or introducing a reform in what is provided for students in a school or college, and make recommendations for future good practice'. Here the project can be based on what you are actually doing at school – the imperative is clear – in this context you are being encouraged to reflect on your ability to plan, evaluate and recommend. Indeed the assessment of such assignments is rooted in the ability to draw on theory and evaluate your own management activity in that context. More recent, of course, is the NPQH. The course is designed to give aspirant headteachers the opportunity to develop the skills and practices they need to lead a school.

We need to think carefully about our own needs as professionals. There is an imperative to grow as a professional, not only in terms of being able to do the job (for example by going on a timetabling course) but also by thinking about leadership issues. Attending conferences (such as the Secondary Heads Association etc.) gives us the opportunity to discuss our work with fellow professionals.

At a local level, too, there are often deputy head groups that offer both support and enrichment. Also, having a mentor (a deputy at another school) is a valued resource that has the advantage of being relatively inexpensive and immediate.

The market place

A further element is that of market awareness. Such a concept is alien to some people's view of education and its purpose, but schools do have this dimension to their role. The way the school presents itself through its prospectus, the branding that accompanies the creation of logos and the like are all important parts of this public face. However, more important is the need for an awareness of market forces and accountability. The impact of OfSTED, league tables and key stage tests, for example, cannot be overstated. It is vital that we recognise the important part that these play in our professional lives. Carol Adams, as Chief Executive of the General Teaching Council, when writing in the *TES* (10 November 2000), compared the news of the resignation of Chris Woodhead with the shooting of Kennedy or the death of Princess Diana although, as she writes, the chief inspector came to be perceived by many teachers as a pantomime villain. His legacy is the central importance of effective teaching and learning in the classroom and, together with effective management, these formed the basis of the inspection framework that has had a significant impact on standards in schools. The world of education now exists in the public forum; the fact that the resignation of Woodhead was headline news is perhaps one example of this. The challenge for us in schools is to move beyond the headlines to what schools need to provide for their students in the twenty-first century. The recent preoccupation with millennium thinking was an appropriate time for us to appraise the past and the impending transition to the information-rich age. The future is, of course, uncertain and the fictional school, Midtown College, envisaged by Bowring-Carr and West-Burnham (1997), may be just around the corner. But public education does have a future. What that future will be is more difficult to say. How can one public education system possibly accommodate all that society needs today, let alone in the future? Our society has become increasingly pluralistic and needs are diverse. However, the mantra is choice: the need for choice, the demand for choice, the provision of choice. But the concept of choice is in itself problematic: we have no choice but to choose.

Faced with the choice of a school for their children, parents have to decide what they want and they have the collective power to scupper a school's prospects. A colleague who is head of a 1,000-student boarding school told me of the effect of public opinion on his school. A shift of emphasis from one of the feeder preparatory schools meant that some fifty children were not sent to his school. The effect of this was to cause a drop in budget of £500,000. Competing schools know only too well that any slight movement in parental preferences can have dramatic effects lasting for years. However, an awareness of local circumstances can bring about dramatic results and involvement in the local community is key to this.

Basic role skills

Job roles and tasks

The environment within which most organisations operate is uncertain and turbulent. Many of today's jobs will be obsolete tomorrow and the skills needed to perform jobs today will not necessarily be needed tomorrow. Schools are no exception to this. Matthew and Tong (1982) write checklists for the pastoral deputy (this term itself is outmoded). The jobs include general oversight of the house/year system, attendance and admission, school meal supervision, school transport, etc. Jobs for the curriculum deputy (Matthew and Tong call the post 'academic' deputy) might include timetable construction and the 'curriculum'. The purpose of this chapter is not to unpick what is meant by either of these job titles, or by the curriculum. However, the list of tasks that form a deputy head's job description has changed because the nature of school management and leadership has changed. In some schools responsibility for the timetable is delegated to a teacher; in one school this task is carried out by a person outside the organisation (whom the school pays about £10,000 to do it). The nature of the tasks to be undertaken by the deputy head is now a function not of their complexity but of their strategic importance.

The traditional skill set for a deputy

For many deputy heads the traditional skill set is redundant and new skills are required. Rather than being present-oriented, we need to look forward and consider what competencies will be required tomorrow. Sparrow and Bognanno (1993) distinguish between four categories of competencies: those that are emerging, maturing, transitional and core. Emerging competencies are those that may not be relevant now but will become so in the future, given the organisation's strategic path. By contrast, maturing competencies are those that have been important to the past success of the organisation (and to jobs within it), but will become less relevant in the future, because of either strategic change or technological obsolescence. Transitional competencies are those that are important neither for current performance nor for the proposed strategic plan, but are vital to the smooth management of change from 'here' to 'there'. (Sparrow and Bognanno suggest that many organisations' 'competencies for change' are really transitional competencies, which may not be required in the longer term. Under this heading they include the capacity to live with uncertainty, to manage stress and to cope with pressure.) Finally, core competencies are those at the heart of effective performance, whose importance is enduring regardless of the vagaries of organisational fashion.

The language of 'competency' in the singular, and 'competences' or 'competencies' in the plural has been one of the 'big ideas' in human resource management in business and industry, on a par with management by objectives, total quality management and empowerment. The principle was that a series of effective individual behaviours are defined, usually in the context of superior organisational performance. This set of behaviours is then operationalised in order to choose the right people to join the organisation, appraise and manage their performance, assess their career readiness or potential, and diagnose appropriate development actions. In a way this was the means of linking effective performance to strategic direction. However, the fundamental weakness in this approach is that it depends entirely on the initial defining process. Applied to school leadership, it meant that the most effective classroom teachers became headteachers because organisational performance could only be measured in terms of an individual class teacher's performance. Thus, the process is flawed, particularly in education, because of a lack of clarity of what competency means: is it vocational (or managerial), behavioural or strategic?

Any definition of competency that attempts to 'describe' focuses first on knowledge, skills and attitudes (and a few personal behaviours). In terms of behavioural competency, a description seeks to explain the behavioural repertoires that people input into a job, role or organisation. However, phrased in terms of the organisation, these are the resources and capabilities of the organisation that link with improved performance. A deputy head needs analytical skill. We live in a data-rich environment: we have information on key stage 2 results (both levels and raw scores), key stage 3 results (teacher assessments, test results) and GCSE results. Add to this the optional tests that will be used for the first time in 2001, the growing use of ability tests (for example, the NFER Cognitive Ability Tests (NFER CAT) and the University of Durham-based YELLIS and ALLIS tests), and there is a huge amount of data available on each pupil, each year group and each school. Much of this information is collected at local level and at national level. Visit the DfEE websites and there is a plethora of statistics about schools over time. This will surely continue and increase as the results of tests become better established.

Talking to a colleague gave me a real insight into the effect of all these statistics. She said that she looks at the stats. If she has time she'll think about looking at the children in her classes but all too often the immediacy of classroom life means that lessons have to be prepared and the data go to the bottom of her work tray. The challenge for me is therefore to present the data in a meaningful and accessible way – and indeed, to have a process or framework that requires a response at all levels in the organisation.

Your challenge as deputy head is not to supply or even create information; it is to analyse the information and make sense of it. The ability to summarise the body of information, make comparisons and present the results to the staff is a crucial one. We want subject leaders and classroom teachers to plan on the basis of information.

All children in Oxfordshire secondary schools take the NFER CAT. The CAT gives a whole raft of information: for example, the NFER CAT gives key stage 3 predictors for the core subjects and GCSE predicted grades for most subjects. However, the data are in the form of these predictors and also raw scores which relate to the verbal, quantitative and non-verbal tests. When you look at the information that arrives from NFER it can be quite daunting. How do you make sense of the data and how can we use them to inform us about the cohort? If you produce tables of information, then people will either give them a cursory glance (and think this is nice, but so what?) or spend time trying to get to grips with what they mean. (Of course, some will disregard them because they don't understand them.) One way to address this is to compare the cohort with the normal population and to produce a graph summarising the data. By producing a graph and providing a commentary to accompany it, you give people the opportunity to consider what the information means to them in their subject. As deputy head, you do the analysis and then ask the questions.

You can then ask people to respond to the graph in front of them (such as the one shown in Figure 6.1). Questions that can be asked include:

- How does the profile for, say, verbal ability compare with the general population?
- If the profile differs from the general population what strategies are required to address this difference?
- If a group has a higher than normal level of quantitative ability, how will this affect the starting points in Mathematics, Science, Technology, etc.?
- What implications does the general profile have for each individual subject?

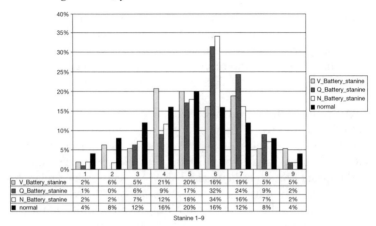

	1	2	3	4	5	6	7	8	9
☐ V_Battery_stanine	2%	6%	5%	21%	20%	16%	19%	5%	5%
■ Q_Battery_stanine	1%	0%	6%	9%	17%	32%	24%	9%	2%
☐ N_Battery_stanine	2%	2%	7%	12%	18%	34%	16%	7%	2%
■ normal	4%	8%	12%	16%	20%	16%	12%	8%	4%

Stanine 1–9

Figure 6.1 Year 7 (1999) stanine distribution for each battery (V, Q, N)

By looking at the information in this way, you start to challenge people's perceptions about the year groups and to encourage them to plan on ability and aptitude. This is sensible use of data that all can engage in.

I discussed this approach with a deputy colleague and his response was that he couldn't do that analysis because he isn't a mathematician and his IT skills were not equal to mine. This attitude has some validity and is understandable. However, the Autumn Package is available on CD-Rom now and it does a lot of the number crunching for us. The PANDA can do much of the analysis for us and we have to respond to it. There are several ways forward if you are unable to do this kind of analysis yourself:

- you can learn, using some of the packages that are available to help or taking a training course
- you engage a colleague with the appropriate skills who can prepare the graphs etc. for you
- you learn to analyse the information that is presented in the PANDA or the Autumn Package and concentrate on this

We are all different and have a varied skill set. If you have IT skills, they can be useful. All school leaders need to be able to analyse data. Actually producing the graph isn't essential, but interpreting it is. Similarly, this analysis is all that is required to set meaningful targets on the basis of information.

Coaching, training and staff development

A further core skill is the ability to coach and train. Scanning the educational press on a Friday evening, I began to reflect on the way in which the content of periodicals such as the *TES* has changed over recent years. Add to this the launch of magazines such as *Managing Schools Today*, the DfEE's *Best of Terms*, and what we have is a cultural shift in what it means to be a professional teacher. If it ever was sufficient to graduate from a university or college, enter the profession and simply do the job, it certainly hasn't been possible to stand still in the tide of educational change over recent years.

All teachers, whatever their role and position in a school, need to keep up to date with their area of expertise and with recent research about pedagogy, if for no other reason than to provide evidence for their Threshold Application. They have to keep up to date with legislative changes that affect their work such as the National Curriculum, assessment, inspection and appraisal. The job has changed significantly over recent years – there is rarely a dissenting voice to that statement – and in this context the function of staff development and the role of the person charged with leading staff development need to be considered.

In this section I want to argue that staff development has to be a process and indeed is a function of school improvement. I regard the role of a staff development manager as fundamentally flawed. What is needed is a radically different approach to this aspect of human resources.

What characterises staff development? For many, staff development means going on courses. While some courses are good, many fail to live up to the promotional literature. How often have we or our colleagues gone on a course and found that the best thing about it, what really made us think, was the conversation with the teacher over coffee? Perhaps this is too harsh. But in seeking to unpick the rationale for staff development, we have to consider what we want it to achieve and how to bring this about.

Starratt (1999) put forward a three-stage model of leadership: transactional, transitional and transformational. This model is useful when considering staff development. If a school is to be transformed, indeed if it is to be capable of being transformed, then it has to be led by people who are capable of personal trans- formation. The leaders of our schools need to bring about cultural change, and that means a change in which the most fundamental aspects of the organisation alter and regrow. It is through this analysis that the process of staff development emerges.

At a basic level, staff development is about making sure that people have the knowledge to do their job. It is about ensuring that people know about changes to the syllabus; are able to deliver the Literacy Hour; know which Shakespeare text to teach Year 9 for the key stage 3 SATs. It is, perhaps, a self-interested exchange: in order to deliver the curriculum, the teachers need to update their knowledge and skills. Although these transactions are self-serving, to the extent that they fulfil the immediate needs of both the organisation and the individual, they are, of necessity, governed by instrumental values such as fairness, contractual commitments and the like. At this level, therefore, the staff development manager has an administrative function, to ensure that the level of activity is commensurate with the curricular change. If the syllabus changes, if the demands of the curriculum alter, there is an immediate need for teachers to update their skills and knowledge. Few would argue with the immediacy of this demand.

However, for the school to make a transformational cultural change, something more radical and creative needs to occur. If people are to be united in the pursuit of communal interests, then they need to be developed as individuals and as groups with common goals. Motivating such collective action are large values such as communal interests (in that if we don't as a school move forward, we go into a spiral of organisational decline), excellence (if we don't seek excellence in ourselves, we can't achieve it in others), equity, social justice and so on. But in order to reach this state, there has to be a transition from the status quo.

In the transitional stage, the school is focused on individual and communal empowerment. Teachers must be included in this endeavour, as a gradual assumption of responsibility for one's actions. This is where the model of 'sending people on courses' falls down. This model has as its basis the principle that we identify a need and send people to a place, a person, or wherever; they have something done to them. This denies any personal responsibility and fails to acknowledge individual professional responsibility, and therefore abstracts the inclusive change that has, of necessity, to occur. For the school to move forward there needs to be a change from passive to active. Teachers have to become responsible for their own development at the individual level. The school needs to be responsible for its collective development at the organisational level. At this stage, the staff development role moves from managerial and transactional to one which is collaborative. This requires co-ordination.

So what kind of activity does the staff development co-ordinator perform now? The name has changed but that will not, in itself, bring about change. The staff development co-ordinator needs to work with groups, perhaps providing training or facilitating developmental activity for groups.

One way in which we could move this forward would be to do some coaching. When we did the lesson observation training, the trainer observed the subject leader giving feedback to the teacher and then gave feedback on the feedback. This was good.

I know when the head has given me feedback on how presentations have gone, how a speech sounded, etc. that I benefited a great deal from his counsel. Perhaps we can build this in.

The staff development co-ordinator needs to work with groups, perhaps providing training or facilitating developmental activity for groups. An example of this might be organising and delivering (in part) middle-management training. This would be characterised by sessions where the function of middle management was aired: the transition from teacher to middle manager was effected. Add to this the creation of whole-staff INSET activities that address the organisation's developmental phase, focusing on, for example, active learning strategies, models of learning and the like. What characterises the activity at this stage is an acknowledgement of competency. The organisation recognises the need for competence and seeks to understand competent practice. All teachers need to develop greater competence in their teaching, whether that involves a broader understanding of their subject matter or greater versatility in motivating their students. So, in this transitional stage, staff development is concerned with the competence of teachers as individuals but also as groups. It is not about what they know (their subject knowledge), but rather about progress from the transactional state to the transformational. This has to pervade the entire organisation; it cannot be just about teachers. For example, you might initiate a detailed programme to develop learning support assistants, in order to ensure that their role is fully integrated into the work of the school, that they are given adequate training, that they contribute to lessons rather than simply turning up and doing whatever seems appropriate at the time. Taken further, the staff development co-ordinator can be the one who distils and promulgates the latest piece of research. One of the more enlightened outcomes of the growth of educational literature has been the dissemination of classroom and school-based research. The staff development co-ordinator takes the research and raises it in the school's conscious mind.

To effect cultural change, there needs to be some kind of transformation. To make it part of the culture of the organisation, there has to be a nucleus that will act both as a steering group and as a consensus-building group. The transformation will only be sustained if it is built on the shared belief that comes from consensus. Typically, the staff development co-ordinator is a deputy head.

This presents the post holder with a unique opportunity to make the change happen. The task can be to identify those who can act as the consensus-building group. Further, the staff development leader co-ordinates the work of smaller groups focused on particular aspects and extensions. As such, staff development becomes a matter of anticipating the changes that will be brought about. To do this the staff development leader focuses on relationships, taking inclusivity as the core purpose. The leader designs activities: the need is determined through enquiry (which is suggested by any or all members of the organisation) and realised through negotiation, collaboration and participation. It means that the staff development leader can go to History department meetings with the brief of coaching the head of History on how to facilitate meetings in a better way. By working alongside the subject leaders, by talking through what they want to achieve from a meeting, by watching them in action and then discussing the outcomes, the co-ordinator develops the role. The cumulative effect of this type of work is that at the personal professional level subject leaders (for example) develop competence in their leadership skill set. At an organisational level, the staff development leader can influence a whole host of people by focusing on the task itself. At this stage the staff development leader becomes both a coach and a consultant; you can challenge and disturb the individual and enable him or her to develop necessary skills. This coaching element could be of huge benefit to the work of individuals and groups.

To achieve this end, however, demands new skills and a change in approach. To empower teachers to bring about professional change through their individual and collective responsibility for the organisation is a strategic and cultural shift. However, it is effective and fulfilling. It relies less on auditing and more on engaging people in the re-creation of their work and their work environment. It is essentially about human significance.

What does this mean for schools today? If they are to transform themselves, then staff development has to be at the heart of what they do. It has to start from a belief that staff development will make a difference, not only at the functional level of knowing what to do, what to teach and how, but, more than this: it means a commitment at all levels of the organisation. It needs to be seen in the context of cultural transformation. As a school progresses and makes its way through the stages outlined above, staff development becomes a paradigm for cultural transformation.

The principle underlying the post of staff development manager is flawed because it fails to acknowledge the task that is required. There is always a need for updating. We all need to know the latest curricular changes and there has to be someone in charge of making sure that we do. However, if articles on, say, seating patterns in classrooms, are to make a difference in schools, someone has to bring these issues to the fore and have the ability to challenge conventional thinking. Moreover, in moving the school forward, the principle has to be one of personal and collective empowerment and responsibility. Moving from manager to co-ordinator to leader means that staff development undergoes its own transformation from functional to fundamental.

Having considered the skills that are inherent in the role of deputy head, I would move on to *core skills* – those aspects that transcend time and strategic choice. By this I include the means to collect information, give information, to generate ideas and sequence actions.

Collecting information

Collecting information is not only about sending out a memo asking how many children are in each teaching group (although this is worth doing periodically to check that the information held on SIMS is correct). It is about collecting information in order to keep the headteacher well informed and to facilitate effective working relationships. If you are responsible for the curriculum (or any aspect of it), then you need to be in a position to comment on the quality of the teaching and learning that is occurring in the school, indeed on any part of it. Some schools have developed their own systems and criteria for lesson observation, but that used by OfSTED is the most useful as it links directly to the inspection process. Being trained to observe and judge lessons using the OfSTED framework is highly beneficial. The ability to assess any lesson at any level is an important one for the deputy head, and one that is frequently overlooked. As a subject leader, for example, you used to observe lessons regularly (see Tranter 2000 for a detailed guide to lesson observation), but only in your own subject. It is different when you are no longer the subject expert.

However, lesson observation is not the only way of collecting information. There are minutes from meetings, outputs from working groups and, of course, the huge amount of information that can be obtained from the SIMS systems. Some of this includes:

- a range of census information about pupils and staff (needed for Form 7)
- absence statistics for particular year groups
- absence statistics for staff
- staff deployment
- cover statistics
- balances of department cost centres
- individual timetables for students
- year timetables

The list seems endless and it is vital that you know how to access this information. Attendance on a SIMS course is therefore a useful adjunct to the professional portfolio.

Giving information

Giving information can be one of the most fraught aspects of the job. You will be told some things that you are not able to share with others. Some of these things will be highly personal and to divulge them would involve a serious breach of confidence. In other cases, perhaps not everyone has yet been asked for their input and so to reveal facts might be premature. Information can be very difficult to control, particularly when the flow has to be one-way. This puts quite a dramatic spin on the business, but so much of your job of being a deputy is about communicating with people effectively. However, one thing is certain: if you are honest at all times, then at best things will be wonderful, at worst they will be as good as they can be. But trying to hide the truth, or attempting to cover something up, never works in the long run. This is especially true of relations with the headteacher. It is my view – and that of all my deputy colleagues – that we must always be absolutely straight with the headteacher and never attempt to cover anything up. All these things are easily said when things are good, but part of being a reflective practitioner is to learn from adversity; this is what makes for principle-centred leadership.

Sequencing actions

Sequencing actions follows on from this. Some deputy heads have the responsibility for the construction of the school timetable and this is a good example of how effective communication and correct sequencing can make the difference between a mess and a success. There are so many constraints and pressures on the timetable and of course it is a very important piece of work. Some of the issues are explored in Table 6.1.

Other tasks in schools are equally demanding. Dealing with difficult children who have been very badly behaved is one example, changing a school policy is another. But it is often personal qualities that make for an effective resolution of any crisis.

What makes a good deputy head?

Earlier in the chapter I asserted that the deputy head is above all things a change agent. The remaining aspect to this is that of personal characteristics: achievement drive and the ability to form relationships.

That you possess achievement drive is self-evident, given the rigours of the recruitment process. But being part of the leadership team is more than that. It is about exploiting opportunities to grow in both personal and professional terms. This can be hard. It is not always easy to see the learning points when things have gone badly, but they are there and persistence and tenacity will sustain you through the difficult times. The deputy head has to be independent: you have to stand with others and also stand alone. To succeed you have to be willing to learn through and in adversity. This is not to say that school is a battleground but there is a sense that many deputies will attest to, of having crossed a line. It is unfortunate when a discussion results in a them/us feeling, but this does happen.

Second is the need for quality relationships. To build these takes time and effort, and cannot be done overnight. In the context of a school, where a year is a short time, you need to think long term rather than short term. Relationships will be right when you are self-aware and listen to what people have to say. There will be times when you are unable to accommodate their wishes, but the fact that you have sought them will be recognised.

Summing up

This chapter is about how you as the deputy head ensure that you grow as a professional in terms of both expertise and competence. The job is very much about effective communication with a wide range of people, but there are specific skills and competences that can be acquired.

You have to acknowledge your need for professional growth. Your skills will need constant updating. This is because the nature of school leadership is constantly changing.

You are, above all, a 'change agent'. There are two types of competence: those aspects of the job that you must carry out effectively and those where you develop particular areas of competence in others.

However, while there are specific areas that you can develop – such as ICT, timetabling, behaviour management – much of the work depends on your ability to coach and develop others. To this end, your role in effecting staff development is key.

What makes for a good deputy head is the ability to learn through adversity and reflect on what has happened. This is a difficult skill to acquire, but will enable you to grow.

Your relationships with all members of the school community and those associated with the school are key. They take time to develop but the willingness to listen and the commitment to building them will transcend many of the difficulties that will inevitably arise.

Table 6.1 An example of a timetable sequence

Phase of timetable process	People affected	Issues
Staffing analysis and curriculum need This is where the current staffing is analysed. Create a spreadsheet with the deployment for each person (for example, subject leaders have more non-contact time than second in departments). Compare this with the curriculum needs – the number of classes, the number of lessons allocated to each subject, etc.	Subject leaders Individual class teachers Senior team head-teacher	Decisions may have to made regarding the viability of groups and sizes of groups Contact ratios are often a source of contention If overall staffing exceeds the curriculum need it might trigger redundancy The vagaries of the resignation process may affect the overall balance Decisions on recruit-ment (particularly for shortage subjects) may have to be made in advance of this analysis
Staffing the timetable Ask subject leaders to indicate who they want to teach each class	Subject leaders Year heads Class teachers	Subject leaders may have particular views on who should teach classes or may need advice on how to staff the subject. If the subject is one where there is setting, the allocation of ability sets can be contentious Heads of year might want input on who will be teaching their year group Class teachers will always have an opinion on which

Phase of timetable process	People affected	Issues
		classes they want, but the deputy head should not be the one to break the news if this does not accord with the subject leaders' views
		The senior team may have a particular view on who should teach which classes – the analysis of results by class teacher can be useful here
First draft of the timetable The first go at the timetable is published	As everyone teaches, this affects all	The constraints on the timetable often mean that compromises have to be made
		Subject leaders may recoil at the thought of their staff teaching Year 9 on Friday afternoon (or whichever year is problematic)
		The distribution of lessons will not suit everyone
		The timetable will be, by no means, completed at this stage and so to raise expectations can be hazardous
The first week of the timetable	The entire school – teachers and students	Will it work and what will happen if it doesn't?

Action points

Professional knowledge:
- know the change process
- understand what motivates those around you
- develop deep knowledge of management and leadership models through reflective practice
- know the educational market place both locally and nationally

Basic role skills:
- analyse the information about the students and the school as a whole
- develop coaching and training skills
- place staff development at the heart of role skills

Core skills:
- Collect information
- analyse information
- give information
- generate ideas
- sequence actions

Characteristics:
- achievement drive – learning in adversity, persistence, independence
- building relationships – being self-aware, persuasive, listening

References and suggestions for further reading

Beare H. (2000) *Creating the Future School* RoutledgeFalmer, London

Bowring-Carr C. and West-Burnham J. (1997) *Effective Learning in Schools* Pearson, London

Glatter R. (ed.) (1989) *Educational Institutions and their Environments: Managing the Boundaries*, Open University Press, Milton Keynes

MacBeath J. and Myers K. (1999) *Effective School Leaders*, Pearson Education, London

Matthew R. and Tong S. (1982) *The Role of the Deputy Head in the Comprehensive School* Ward Lock Educational, London

Matthewman M. (2000) *Examination Results: Processing, Analysis and Presentation* RoutledgeFalmer, London
At the beginning of each academic year schools are required to present their examination results. This A4 book and disk provides clear guidance for examination officers on how to process, analyse and record these results.

Richards C. and Taylor P. (eds) (1998) *How Shall We School Our Children?* RoutledgeFalmer, London

Sparrow P.R. and Bognanno M. (1993) 'Competency Requirement Forecasting: Issues for International Selection and Assessment' *International Journal of Selection and Assessment*, **1**, 50–58

Starratt R. (1999) 'Moral Dimensions of Leadership' in Begley P. and Leonard P. (1999) *The Values of Educational Administration*, RoutledgeFalmer, London

Tranter S. (2000) *From Teacher to Middle Manager – Making the Next Step* Pearson, London

7   Too much to do?

Thursday, 31 May

Things to do today:

1   Organise checking of set lists on SIMS.
2   CPG agenda.
3   Ask secretary to ring up primary schools — are they coming to the meeting?
4   PG's job description?
5   HW — money for books.
6   Cancel meeting with JW.
7   Print target setting doc. for SMT.
8   See PA about Jonathan East.
9   Why was Sarah Beau out of school yesterday??

Briefing this morning — remind everyone about cover.

•   Remind head to thank for Year 9 parents' evening.

8.45 — Teach Year 11
9.45 — Meeting with AP — Schemes of work, long-term plans for Music.
10.45 — REMEMBER BREAK DUTY.
11.05 — Teach Year 12.
12.05 — Lesson observation — sports hall — use of group work is focus.
1.05
1.55 — Year 10 assembly.

2.15 – Meet headteacher—weekly meeting.
3.30 – Assessment working party.

Thinking about all that I have to do
tomorrow. There are some very big issues
that I have to deal with. If I classify
these tasks they fall into a number of
categories.

1	Library supervision
2	Subject review policy
3	Numbers in Year 9 – are we OK?
4	GCSE entry policy
5	Specialist school status??
6	JL's lesson was awful
7	Rooming for next year??

Immediate

- Print target setting doc. for SMT.
- See P.A about Jonathan East.
- Why was Sarah Beau out of school yesterday??
- Cancel meeting with JW.

Administrative

- Organise checking of set lists on SIMS.
- Ask secretary to ring up primary schools – are they coming to the meeting?
- CPG agenda

My teaching

Leading strategic change:

a. GCSE entry policy
b. Meeting with heads of departments
c. PG's job description?
d. Subject review policy

Thinking ahead

a. Rooming for next year??
b. Specialist school status

Quality assurance

a.   Lesson observation – sports hall – use of group work is focus

There is a lot to do today and it's all essential. But there are no spaces for me to do all of these things that need to be done. I have too much to do. I remember talking to Gordon when I was at the deputy heads meeting yesterday and he was saying that he gives his classes work to get on with so that he can do some of his admin. But I'm responsible for the quality of teaching and learning at this school – I have to be seen to be teaching to a high standard all the time – so even if I wanted to do this, I can't.

I'm going to have to give this some thought – the more I set up, the more I aim to sort out, the more I have to do.

I need to think about how I can delegate to others.

I need to think about how I can lead strategic change so that I work with people rather than direct them all the time.

When I see the head I'll talk to him about how I can work with people in a more proactive manner – but how can I keep track of everything that other people do??? Last week he showed me The Art of War by Sun Tzu – that was about how to build an organisation using the talents of others.

One of the many skills that you must acquire and practise assiduously as a new deputy is the ability to delegate effectively. Making the transition from the middle-management role to that of deputy means fundamentally a loss of control and, perhaps less worryingly, a change in the nature of control. But delegation also requires a consideration of the nature of responsibility and accountability. At an early stage in the role, it can be difficult to let go of tasks when you know you will be held to account for them.

A common area of responsibility for deputies is to lead a middle-management team, usually comprising subject leaders or heads of year, sometimes a blend of both. However, the fact that many of us will have been promoted through this route will give us ideas on how we want things to be done but may expose us in other ways.

The degree of control we are able to or wish to exert over our assigned areas says something about us. But if you try to run the year team through the head of year, then you miss an opportunity to develop individuals. Further, the organisation will at best be wholly dependent on you and at worst be unable to function without you. You need to invest in people and use the task culture to develop their skills.

This is another way in which the role of the deputy head has changed significantly; we still have an operational and a functional aspect to our work but we also need to think in strategic terms and, indeed, to lead strategic change. But with this emphasis on people and their needs comes that modern phenomenon – stress. What is healthy encouragement and pressure for one person might be an unbearable strain for another. As school leaders, we have a moral and legal responsibility to take this into account.

For heads of department, it is possible to exert a fair degree of control over the work of the team. The subject is delivered in a designated area – the subject teachers work in a group of classrooms all located close together. For me, the remit was to teach Mathematics – and as such my work was all about teaching Mathematics. It was my job, as head of the subject, to know, and be able to speak with authority on, such matters as the syllabus, the board, the procedures – all manner of things mathematical. What went on in every Mathematics classroom was my concern. It was my job to ensure that Mathematics was taught the right way, at the right time and to the right level. How different the job of deputy was to be!

An important part of the job of the deputy with responsibility for the curriculum is to be able to speak with confidence about these matters – for all subjects. I received a phone call in the first fortnight from a parent who wanted to know our rationale for the curriculum structure we operate. There is no easy way to prepare for these sorts of questions. An important part of the culture of an open organisation is that people can ask questions at any time.

Working with subject leaders

My model of operation with subject leaders is to hold regular meetings with them. I started off by doing a sort of fact find. I asked them to complete a pro forma where they commented on their results over the past three years. I also asked them to describe any changes that had occurred over recent years. This was my way into their subject. As a newly appointed deputy, you may worry, however, about how to discuss, say, French pedagogy, when the last time you studied the subject was when you were in Year 11 at school. I wondered how I could possibly say anything useful to subject experts about their subject. However, after some discussion with the headteacher and fellow deputies (who were more experienced), I came to the view that this wasn't what was required. If I had tried to talk with authority on, say, History methodology, then at best I might say something useful but, at worst, I'd look foolish. What is required, however, is the ability to facilitate discussion and challenge accepted subject practices. Subject-specific advice and information are, of course, available from subject advisers (for example, LEA advisers). Also, the necessary immersion in the curriculum does give one a particular insight in that we can see what happens across different subjects and identify the links that might be exploited to advantage.

The constant drive for higher standards and increased levels of performance often raises the concern that focusing on the jobs that have to be done means that the people who do them are neglected. Most people have, at some time, felt that their employer has failed to recognise them as a person, seeing them merely in terms of their job role. Indeed a measure of detachment is important if the manager – at whatever level – is to carry out his or her own tasks. The caring side of management is often seen as incompatible with

---

When I started as a deputy I thought that getting the job done was the most important thing. I've worked really hard to make sure that things have gone to plan. But there's a lot of talent in the school that perhaps I'm not maximising. Instead of thinking of what needs to be done I could think more about who is the best person to do the job or how I could work with a group to get the work done. I'm thinking less about the tasks and more about the people.

the demand for the assiduous monitoring that has become part of the brief of many a manager in schools today.

People in a task culture

In this chapter I want to argue that the individual can be at the fore in the task culture, but this requires a different manner of operation. Starting a new job in a new school gives you a clarity of purpose that cannot be wasted. We arrive at our new school full of experience of one organisation but no experience of new one. It is to be hoped that we see things that those who have been in the school for a long time miss; that is the strength of the recruitment and promotion practice in schools today. So you can start the management of your job by thinking about the tasks that have to be done. Think about what needs to be done. Break down the aims of the school into the constituent parts and translate them into measurable outcomes and definable tasks and roles. You have to organise, manage, monitor, evaluate and review.

But if this process becomes self-perpetuating, you miss an opportunity. You might think that the business of sustained school improvement starts with tenacious dedication to the completion of these clearly articulated and well-defined tasks, but you would thereby neglect the opportunity to move further. An organisation, to enjoy sustained growth, needs to develop maturity. It has to move from a process of transactions – where the manager defines the task and determines the outcomes – to one where the organisation becomes the force that brings about lasting change for itself.

How does this happen? One way in which this lasting and more pervasive change can be brought about is to move from task investment to person investment. Instead of devoting the interaction time on what the job is, what has to be done, what the steps are, how it will be measured, etc., move on to an interaction which focuses on changing the way in which a person thinks about his or her job. The dynamic is to challenge thinking. You have to ask: what is the point of my job? This relies heavily on skilled facilitation of meetings where the focus is on the task through the efforts of the person who actually has to undertake the task. For example, in setting an exam timetable for a year group, the likely people to be involved are the exam officer, the head of year and the curriculum manager. In my particular school, the exam officer organises the exams, the head of year is responsible for the academic progress of the year group, the curriculum manager ensures that the curriculum is delivered in a coherent way, and the deputy headteacher has line responsibility for the curriculum in its entirety. It would be possible for all the people involved in this exercise to put forward their own views in a combative manner, fighting for their own interests. The exams officer might organise the timetable to complete the task in the shortest time possible, with a high level of supervision, so that the task gets completed quickly and with sufficient staffing to ensure that few problems arise. The remit of the head of year is to ensure that the students have adequate time and space between their exams to revise and manage their own pressures. She may argue that spreading the exams over a two-week period, with students on study leave, will enable them to do their best in a relaxed atmosphere. The curriculum manager may be focusing on how the exams are managed to ensure that there is time for staff to mark the papers, make proper assessments and set targets for the students and subject teams. For these purposes, the core subjects should be done first, and the timetable should be arranged so that minimum time is taken out of lessons, with as few staff as possible (so that remaining staff can be used for any cover). The deputy head, faced with all of these concerns, has to manage the process in such a way that all concerns are met as far as possible. The task on the face of it is simple, and a common one. However, these sorts of things can raise a number of issues that require consideration.

But the headteacher will want me to be able to say what's going on and I need to be sure that things work the way I want them. I'm responsible for what happens and I have to be accountable for what occurs.

The first is the nature of responsibility and accountability. Who is responsible for the exams? On the face of it, in this situation, the exams officer. It is his job to sort out all the arrangements for the exam period. The organisation of the premises, setting up the desks, timetables and all the associated tasks – they are all part of the exam officer's remit. One could argue that the job is about making sure that the exams happen at the required time. But the nature of school life is such that the logistical implications of a particular task are not the sole consideration. Working in a school is about managing groups of people, whether aged 15 or the teaching staff. The work of a school is not confined to the practical considerations of the job. People's feelings also have to be recognised. So, back to this exam timetable: the head of year has a responsibility to the school for ensuring that the children do their best and she also has a moral responsibility to represent the students' interests by ensuring that they get the 'best deal'. For the curriculum manager, the person responsible for the progress of the school population, the concerns may be somewhat less personal. It is quite difficult to unpick these notions, and in many ways this is what makes leading a school so much more exciting than running a baked bean factory. In our schools we have a wide audience; our respondents are the students, their parents, the staff, the governors, the local community – the list goes on. The task of exam timetabling could seem quite simple but if you only focus on the operational aspects of the job, you lose the opportunity to develop the people you depend on to make things happen. By adopting an approach that focuses on the people as having an investment in the task, then a more creative dynamic ensues. This type of facilitation will bring about ownership of the task and reflect the values of the organisation to a greater degree. If the values of the organisation are sufficiently embedded in the people, then their vision will be realised because of their strength of purpose.

This is not easy. It demands a risk-taking environment. It requires a different kind of management, one not focused entirely on tasks but reliant on people for its inspiration. This could be the key to sustained school improvement. Many of us have wondered how it is that a bright, enthusiastic newly qualified teacher can have become the staffroom cynic twenty years later. We have wondered how the sad and bored head of subject ever persuaded a panel to appoint him. If we knew which day it happened, which incident changed the individual's view, then we could, perhaps, change things. But to do so, we have to have a culture that sees people as the organisation. There has to be an understanding of the mesh that is school life; someone may be the head of Botany, for example – but is also a member of a subject team, a classroom teacher, a pastoral tutor and so on. Indeed, the multifarious nature of school interrelationships is often the stuff of drama and comedy combined. To invest in people means to see them as the essential components of the organisation. They are the fibres that make up the fabric of the school. By making the move from the task to the person, we achieve so many things: we create a climate where each person is inextricably linked to the organisation. Also, our perception deepens: our awareness of the fragility of the people who work in our schools is enhanced. We see people not as functionaries, who can be directed to do this and that; rather, we see each person as an agent of change, charged with his or her own future.

Leading strategic change

One aspect of your job as deputy headteacher is to lead strategic change. A leader of a subject team or indeed a pastoral group may be parochial. The concerns of a head of Mathematics are legitimately those that pertain to teaching and learning issues in Mathematics. In many ways, this is what is expected of subject leaders: they fight their own corner, they defend their own interests, they look to themselves to solve their own problems and address the issues that affect them in their area. This is one of the more challenging transitions for the deputy headteacher. No longer can you control every aspect of the work (if you ever believed you could) but the enormity of the task that defines being a school leader means that to attempt it would be folly.

Why attempt it? Do you lack trust in others to do the job? This is possible. There are countless stories of people who persist in their belief that they can do it all. Some of them believe that their way is right and nothing else will do. Some believe that 'by the time' the task is explained they could have done it themselves. Some won't let go.

To adopt this approach as deputy head is fundamentally flawed. It is foolish because in trying to do everything, you inevitably end up doing a wide range of tasks, from ordering the flowers for the Open Day display, to writing the exam timetable and creating the school development plan. Some of the tasks within this range are things that it is appropriate for the deputy head to do. Some of the things that the headteacher and I regularly do include picking up litter, putting out chairs for the staff meeting, and making tea for the governors. It would be inappropriate for us to ask staff to pick up litter but by doing it ourselves, hopefully we encourage others to do it too. We might be able to arrange for the site staff to put out chairs for the staff meeting, but it will have to be us if there's something else that needs their attention. To create a dichotomy between the staff and 'us' is perhaps unhealthy and not in the interests of effective whole-team strategy but there is a point that most deputies and heads will recognise: we do certain things because no one else can be asked to do them. It's not that we are the only people who could do these things; it's more that we are the only people who will do them. But if we spend our time doing all these things, we lose the opportunity to concentrate on more strategic work.

What is strategic change?

The whole notion of strategic change and, indeed, of change itself has altered considerably in recent years. Fullan (1987) emphasised the need for studying the dynamics of curriculum change (in particular) in order to make the process more explicit. There are three stages to the change process:

1   Initiation: this is where the need is linked to the agenda. There should be a plan of what the change will be and whom it will involve. Further, in this context there should exist a commitment, and therefore an advocacy, for the change.

2   Implementation: the manager needs to orchestrate the change, balancing pressure and support.
3   Institutionalisation: for change to be effective, the new procedures need to become part of the fabric of the organisation.

Generally, the dominant model of change was one where the process was managed from inception, through planning, to realisation. However, the concept of change itself has undergone some moderation. The golden age where things stayed the same for a long period of time is over (and I would not call it a golden age). We have to cultivate change because it is all around us: there is no steady state; there is no time when things ever stand still.

However, change management still requires these fundamental skills:

- recognising the need for change
- planning for change
- managing change
- reviewing the change and setting new goals.

It is perhaps the word 'goal' that underlies the importance of a new mode of thinking on change. The concept of organisational goals holds a powerful attraction for both leaders and theorists. One of the distinguishing characteristics of organisations as social units is that they are established for specific purposes. There can be no possible doubt that schools are established for the purpose of educating the young, and school goals incorporate this purpose. The achievement of these goals is our *raison d'être*. The headteacher proclaims the goals of the school in the school brochure, in the staff handbook and to the assembled guests on speech night. Goals give a meaning to what the school does. Organisational theorists, or those of a functionalist persuasion, find the concept of a goal a useful aid to understanding organisational processes. Goals provide a focus for their enquiries and enable them to judge the contribution of a particular activity to the whole. If goals can be operationalised they provide the yardstick whereby the effectiveness of an organisation can be judged both on its own terms or from a comparative view.

Leadership is the buzzword of the moment. It is about creating a sense of purpose and direction, and ensuring that there is alignment between the two. Moreover, it is about inspiring people to achieve. As part of the school leadership team, you must look forward and create the framework in which people can be inspired to succeed. But creating and sustaining this vision is not easy. There has been a movement, as illustrated in the previous discussion, to move towards an 'investment in people' culture rather than focusing precisely on the task that has to be completed.

Different strategies appear to have differing implications for the significance of people in the organisation. There is a fundamental question here for the school leader: under what circumstances are people critical success factors? A simple answer might be 'always'. In a different context Prahald and Hamel (1990) have argued that rather than treat the organisation as a collection of strategic business units to be developed or divested according to market conditions, long-term product leadership is gained from viewing the organisation as a portfolio of core competence carriers over the long term. Many in education would probably give a comparable answer. Schools are organisations that depend on people to make them work; or, put more fundamentally, a school only exists by virtue of people. It exists for the people and is the people. A model for strategic change is presented by Williams and Dobson (1997) and is analysed in Table 7.1 in relation to school leadership. The three strategies they describe are innovation, quality enhancement and cost reduction.

Strategic change will typically require the school to revise its person specifications dimensions and methods of selection in order to provide for future manpower requirements. In aligning selection to strategy in this way, selection can act as a significant agent for change.

The challenge of the twenty-first century

How to bring all this about is perhaps the greatest challenge of school leadership. The context for this change is perhaps best explained by Barber (2000) in his description of the challenge of

Table 7.1 A model for strategic change and its relationship with school leadership

Strategy	Employee role behaviour	Human Resources Management policies	Some thoughts on school leadership
Innovation	A high degree of creative behaviour Longer-term focus A relatively high level of co-operative, interdependent behaviour A moderate concern for quality A moderate concern for quantity An equal degree of concern for process and results A greater degree of risk taking A high tolerance of ambiguity and unpredictability	Jobs that require close interaction and co-ordination among groups of individuals Performance appraisals that are more likely to reflect longer-term and group-based achievements Jobs that allow employees to develop skills that can be used in other positions in the school Compensation systems that emphasise internal equity rather than external or market-based equity Broad career paths to emphasise the development of a broad range of skills	The implication of the employee role behaviour and HRM policies is that we need to develop and sustain an organisation that promotes that co-ordination and interaction. This is, essentially, effective team strategy However, with the new performance management system, there is an emphasis on individual contributions to team performance. We have to guard against losing sight of the corporeal nature of school improvement. It has to balance individual performance of teachers with a whole-school response to sustained improvement Schools are often places where people spend a very large part

Table 7.1 (continued)

Strategy	Employee role behaviour	Human Resources Management policies	Some thoughts on school leadership
			of their working lives (working for over ten years in one school is not untypical). Therefore, we have to create a climate where schoolteachers can develop a range of skills that will enable them to move from one role to another; this will go some way to sustaining the motivation of the individual and enhancing the creative opportunities for the school Perhaps we need to view the career in teaching in broader terms: when we recruit to promoted posts, perhaps look for people who have breadth of experience (for example, a faculty head should have pastoral experience too)

Table 7.1 (continued)

Strategy	Employee role behaviour	Human Resources Management policies	Some thoughts on school leadership
Quality enhancement	Relatively repetitive and predictable behaviours A longer-term or more intermediate focus A moderate amount of co-operative, interdependent behaviour A high concern for quality A modest concern for quantity of output High concern for process Low risk-taking activity Commitment to the goals of the school	Relatively fixed and explicit job descriptions High levels of participation in decisions relevant to immediate work conditions and the job itself A mix of individual and group criteria for performance appraisal that is mostly short term and result oriented Extensive and continuous training and development of employees	There needs to be a commonality, a sense of 'custom and practice', so that the benefits that come from change are maximised and are not lost in the drive to move forward The phrase 'singing from the same hymn sheet' comes to mind here. However, the importance of whole staff involvement in major decision making cannot be overstated. Using staff meeting time to work in cross-phase groups is a way of generating and collecting ideas and strategies on how the school can progress One opportunity presented by performance management is to set targets which relate to individual performance and also collective performance. For example, members of the

Table 7.1 (continued)

Strategy	Employee role behaviour	Human Resources Management policies	Some thoughts on school leadership
			Science team may have the department target as part of their individual objectives. To achieve this will require effective teamwork and collective responsibility
Cost reduction	Relatively repetitive and predictable behaviour A rather short-term focus Primarily autonomous or individual activity Moderate concern for quality High concern for quantity of output Primary concern for results Low risk-taking activity Relatively high degree of comfort with stability	Relatively fixed and explicit job descriptions that allow little room for ambiguity Narrowly designed jobs and narrowly defined career paths that encourage specialisation, expertise and efficiency Minimal levels of employee training and development	Schools are expensive places to run and there never seems to be enough money. As school leaders we have to look for ways in which we can reduce costs while sustaining growth. The imperative of individual focus becomes evident here.

the twenty-first century. Historically, public education systems were the product of decisive forces of the nineteenth century – industrialisation and the nation-state. Education was very much the means whereby the population was prepared to make its contribution to the industrial society. In a way, this was what shaped national identity. Nineteenth-century society was clearly stratified by social class. Purvis (1984) quotes the lines from the hymn 'All Things Bright and Beautiful':

> The rich man at his castle
> The poor man at his gate
> God made them high and lowly
> And ordered their estate.

As these lines illustrate, social class differentiation was often supported by the belief that this was part of the divine order. The education of children in the nineteenth century reflected this differentiation. For the great majority of English children in the 1950s and 1960s the 11-plus was the first (and in many cases the last) public examination they took. Children took three papers, in Mathematics, English Language and General Intelligence. The Mathematics paper involved simple addition, subtraction and so on. General intelligence was about the recognition of order in the symbolic world: numbers and patterns in sequence constituted the test. After about one and a half hours the die was cast for children and their educational fate was sealed. Evans (1991) describes how 'it was make or break on that one day'. Barber (2000) argues that as the twenty-first century begins the case for public education needs restating because, if its rationale is unclear, it is in danger. The consequences of economic growth are both a rise in disposable incomes and an appreciation of what it takes to maintain it. No longer will people accept the education they received as suitable for their own children. They want something better, or at least something different. They don't want their children to 'suffer' the educational experience that they had. It is perhaps worth reflecting on this aspect of our parent profile. The last twenty years of the twentieth century saw periods of incredible growth. Economies boomed; the incomes of the few became the incomes of many more. No longer was a high level of income commensurate with a high-status job. People became wealthy sometimes by virtue of the house they lived in. Later, people became wealthy by winning vast sums on a National Lottery. There developed a sense that the high-income jobs were accessible to all, given the right education (for example, the poor child could go to university and become a doctor, lawyer, stockbroker, etc.). But failing that, a lottery ticket could achieve the high income. The growth of middle England has given people an increased awareness of what can be achieved. Add to this a Labour government whose mantra was 'Education, Education, education' and the defining purpose of education is no longer subjected to market forces determined by privilege and class alone. Parents might decide to spend their income on buying an education tailored to their view of the world.

> Thought about this on the way home. I was talking to Julie and she is finding it really hard to cope with her Year 9 Italian class. They seem to be very noisy and she was very upset at the end of school today. They are an able class according to their baseline test results, but she seems to be having a lot of difficulty with them. She looks very stressed. Looking at the absence statistics she has had 12 days off since September – all fairly minor, but I think I will need to have a longer chat with her to see if we can work on this together.

Barber (2000) argues that a good education system is increasingly important not only to the success of a modern economy but also to the creation of a just society. In the twentieth century most educators believed this to be true but few education systems delivered the universal standards it implied. But this didn't matter. People could get unskilled and semi-skilled jobs. If people left school not having received a quality education, they could still go to work, they could make a life for themselves. As school leaders what are we to do? We recognise the educational debate, but we want to know what to do about it. But our purpose is to bring about creating the just society that we all crave and we have to make the change that brings this about. We have to recognise that there is no steady state and that any pretension that we will reach the golden age when all is done is illusory – but with this comes a price.

Stress in the workplace

We hear about organisational and occupational stress at regular intervals. Teacherline recently reported (*TES*, 10 November 2000) that many stressed-out staff were ringing the help number to complain about the relentless rate of change that characterises the typical school today. Dealing with change is therefore a key skill. Recognising stress is another. Under the Health and Safety at Work Act (1974) employers have a duty to ensure the health, safety and welfare at work of all their employees; under Management of Health and Safety and Work Regulations (1992) employers have the duty to assess the health and safety risks to which their employees are exposed at work. This is a major issue for school leaders, especially those leading a school undergoing considerable change and requiring a high level of response.

> Finished late this evening. Before taking this job I was at the gym every night. The enormity of what I have to do means that I don't get to go that often. Sometimes it's because of evening meetings, sometimes because I have a lot of work to do; sometimes I'm just too tired.

For the deputy headteacher, stress operates at two levels. One has to manage one's own levels of stress and those of others. One of the things I was concerned about when I took on the role of deputy head was how the job might change me both in terms of my lifestyle and in terms of the way I saw my work. I was discussing this recently with a colleague, Simon. What started this discussion was Simon describing how he had dealt with an incident involving Louise, a member of his teaching staff. This normally reliable member of staff had forgotten to do her bus duty and it was reported to the deputy head. So Simon sent for Louise. He ended up being unpleasant and what should have been a straightforward matter resulted in an acrimonious meeting with Louise upset. Describing this event to me, Simon seemed almost pleased with himself. When I made this observation his response was that he was always nasty to everyone now. I thought this very sad because it means that he has lost sight of what is important and of any perspective that he once had. It is true that we all have times when we feel cross and irritated, but it is part of our job to ensure that we don't fall victim to the 'hard cop' culture that this incident illustrates. However, the sharpness of the role of deputy head is not without its pressures.

A deputy colleague, Jane, is responsible for managing the cover at her school. She has a tight budget for managing this aspect of school life. A normally very placid person, she told me of a day that caused her to display uncharacteristic levels of annoyance, indeed anger. She had spent a considerable amount of time organising supply cover for the following day. Staff had been complaining about the amount of cover they were being required to do. There was considerable pressure on Jane to manage this issue. So she spent a good deal of time arranging supply cover, ending up employing a teacher via an agency charging a very high rate. However, the next day, two staff returned to work, but didn't let her know. She found out that the supply cover was not needed when she went to the staffroom and saw the teachers at their communication post. What was she to do? Sending the supply teacher home would still cost the school. Jane described how she felt at this time: 'I was so angry. I felt that all my efforts were in vain. I thought that the head would be really angry and that I looked incompetent.'

It would be useful for you to think what you would do under these circumstances. It would be understandable to get very cross with the people concerned. But I think most serving deputy headteachers would resist this. You have to embody high levels of professionalism and ensure that your standards of conduct are exemplary.

The second aspect to this is the effect on your personal life. Certainly, much is demanded of school leaders. There are school events that you have to attend. It may go unnoticed if the head of Mathematics isn't at the school concert, but not if you, the deputy head, do not appear. Combine this with governors' meetings, parent–teacher meetings, consultation evenings and the like, and there is a significant out-of-hours commitment to the role. Of course, attending a governors' meeting means that the time you would spend doing the rest of the job gets pushed into the small hours. The difficulty of managing a big role, with the need for attendance (the 'being there' factor), can put you under considerable pressure. How can you do it? Time affects us all. It is part of the social ethos of everyday experiences. In schools, time is often seen as something to be managed, almost as a commodity. Indeed to some extent it is, since the way we use our time has financial implications. Although time in school, as an organisational construct, is calendar based and looks towards the future, when children take exams, when school terms finish and the like, it is also about what we strive to do in the hours that make up a school day. There is a sense in which time confers status and power to an individual.

To teach or not to teach?

Headteachers either teach or they don't. I discussed the question of whether heads should teach with a serving headteacher and she said that the reason that she didn't teach was because her job was to lead and manage the school. She could execute this responsibility best through devoting her time and energy to it. If straw polls are anything to go by, most staffroom surveys would not support that view. However, in seeking a deputy head post I was surprised at the level of non-contact time that deputies receive, varying from about 20 to 50 per cent. (Indeed the word 'receive' reflects a central tenet of this debate.) The levels of non-contact time in secondary schools (and to a lesser extent in primary schools) can be a source of considerable disquiet. The objective notion of time, as a commodity, is value laden for a school leader. Should school leaders teach classes and why?

In my discussions at various times, three reasons for teaching are often cited:

1   So that you know what's going on. The implication here is, obviously, that if you don't teach then you don't know what's going on. I think there is some validity to this argument. As school leaders, we have to finds ways of 'knowing'. We have to have that in-depth knowledge of the school that will enable us to challenge existing practice from the basis of informed opinion. But, given the enormity of the job of managing a school, how much knowledge can you get from teaching a class of thirty, four times a week? Would you find out more by walking around the school four times a week or acting as a classroom assistant for those four periods? These are questions that we can only answer from our own school perspective. However, to rely on teaching one class to 'know what's going on' is perhaps a rather narrow perspective.

2   So that you know what it's like to be a classroom teacher. In most schools, it would be unusual to find a class taught by the headteacher that wasn't well behaved. To a lesser extent, the same is true for the deputy head. So the question arises: to what extent is the experience of teaching a class contingent on status? Does the deputy head (or school leader for that matter) really know what it is like to be teaching on a 75 per cent or more teaching contact timetable. For example, if you have had to deal with a student in a disciplinary situation that has involved exclusion, it is unlikely that he or she will be badly behaved on returning to class, knowing that you have the power to exclude. Put simply, children know the hierarchy and are not going to expose themselves in this way.

3   You should do cover to take the pressure off staff. This is an old chestnut. The argument is that the amount of cover done should be in proportion to the amount of free time one has. Therefore, a school leader on a 25 per cent contact timetable might do three times the amount of cover that a colleague on a 75 per cent contact timetable does. There might be occasions and circumstances where this is desirable. However, to pay a school leader to do cover is economically foolhardy.

The job is to lead the school

Your job as school leader is to lead the school. This doesn't mean that you don't do other things – teaching, cover, duties and the like – but rather that your involvement is measured and considered in a rational manner. Moreover, the reasons for what you do (or don't do!) must be made explicit. The conferment of time to do a job is seen as a privilege – the more power you have, the more time you have. The way in which an organisation confers 'time privilege' can be seen as a reflection of the importance of a role. Moreover, the way in which we use time is a reflection of the quality of our life. Our views of time and the decisions we make about our use of time are integrally connected to what we value and what we believe. Lafleur (1999) refers to being a 'victim of circumstance'. He asserts that we find ourselves in time binds that define our day-to-day existence and limit our freedom to be ourselves. Consider, for example, the teacher whose time is increasingly colonised by administrative tasks, or the principal who must spend time implementing a number of mandated educational changes without sufficient resources and support. In these instances, our efforts to practise what we value are warped by time. Tensions, anxiety, frustration and stress are common features of today's hectic pace of living. There is, necessarily, a tension between what we want to do (both professionally and personally) and what we have to do. But there are ways to manage this aspect of our lives and to reconcile wants and needs.

However, in order to make sense of time, we do need to consider it in a new way. It is true that it is a resource, to be consumed and invested. Giving our time to something suggests that we value it. The things which we don't value we don't spend time on. Or is this too simplistic? Alternatively we can view how time is spent as an opportunity to challenge existing ways of working. Too often, when teachers prepare resources for use with their classes, these hastily constructed worksheets (to take the most extreme case, expressed in the most pejorative terms) will have a useful life of exactly one lesson. In some cases, teachers struggle to prepare them. In many schools the busiest place first thing in the morning is the photocopying room where reams of paper are used. And to what end? Would it be better if resources were planned? Would it be better if a worksheet was created collaboratively and produced as a resource that everyone could use? But, of course, this would take time and where would the time come from? Too much time is spent by teachers planning lessons – or thinking about what they are going to do with their classes. How much better it would be if there were lesson-by-lesson objectives. The benefit would be to ensure that the curriculum was covered and to free teachers to spend their time assessing students' work and collaborating to produce quality resources. It is by adopting a strategic stance in relation to these fundamentals that time is created. In this era, we have to look for ways to maximise opportunities for collaboration and minimise time spent working alone. There is a paradox in this argument that we can create time in a climate of colonisation by government and management strategy. However, although this is a management strategy to colonise the way in which the curriculum is specified (for example), it is a leadership paradigm that creates and sustains school transformation. A school curriculum is planned, organised and resourced through the efforts of the subject teams. The spin-offs are greater investment by the teachers who have created the curriculum, an effective monitoring tool and, of course, organisational efficiency.

Coping with the job: a value model

But to return to the issue of the deputy as a person, how do you learn to cope with all the work? So much of this is about values and commitment to the school culture and a belief that it can work. Hodgkinson (1999) refers to a tripartite model of values: Type III (preference values), Type II (consensus and consequence values) and Type I (principle values). In this context, Type III values are what we prefer as individuals and what we enjoy doing. So if we prefer data analysis and target-setting strategies, then all is well. They are rooted in our emotions and are affective. We feel good about doing these things, about working on this project, because it is intrinsically enjoyable. Type IIb values are rooted in what is right and what ought to be. We do the data analysis because we think it is right for us to do it and we think that we ought to do it. Type IIa values are also concerned with what is right, but they presuppose a social context with social norms. In this context, we do the data analysis because the social context in which we work means that we believe it is right for us to do the work, and the organisation in which we work confirms that we ought. Type I values are grounded in the metaphysical; principles dominate. They require an act of faith or commitment. We do the data analysis because we are committed to what it will bring about and we have faith in what we do. This enables us to commit ourselves to the jobs we do. In many ways this is where school leadership becomes all-encompassing. It requires commitment to the role, not just to the job. How we perceive and use our time involves some hard choices. Making decisions is largely value-based. How we perceive time, how we construct time and how we use time provides, in Lafleur's terms, 'a lens for seeing who we are and what we value'. The existing mandated structure of the school day, the school curriculum and the multitude of administrative tasks and never-ending demands may make us feel that we cannot exert any measure of control. But as school leaders we can create spaces where others can work collaboratively and productively. But what we cannot do is pretend that the job is anything other than one that requires sustained effort. That there has been change and confusion in education is largely irrelevant. It merely provides a context for principled judgement to be exercised. Values determine purpose and policy; they give direction and motivation to human activity.

Summing up

Effective delegation is an important part of your job. However, it means that you have to find ways of monitoring the work of the school so that you know what is going on, without doing all the work yourself. Regular meetings with key staff, where the outcomes are recorded as minutes, are one way of achieving this. You keep the headteacher informed of your work by giving him or her copies of these documents.

Staff development is an important dimension to your role as deputy head and this represents a shift of emphasis from the task culture to one that focuses on the person. The investment is in the person rather than the task and we achieve this by challenging people's thinking.

Leading strategic change is a vital dimension of your function and this is one of the greatest challenges that schools face. The demands of the job are considerable and being a principle-centred leader is fundamental. Values are inviolate.

Action points

- Develop systems where you are able to record the outcomes of meetings.
- Develop the means to keep the headteacher informed of your work.
- Staff development is the key to organisational and cultural change.
- Think people investment rather than task investment.
- Change management is about recognising the need for change, and planning, managing and reviewing.
- Develop your own perspective on leadership.
- Consider your principles and values.
- Think about your stress management strategies: as deputy you have a responsibility for managing stress in the workplace.

References and suggestions for further reading

Barber Michael (2000) 'The Challenge of the 21st Century' *Times Educational Supplement* 3 November 2000

Evans M. (1991) 'Culture and Class' in Blair M., Holland J. and Sheldon S. (eds) *Identity and Diversity: Gender and the Experience of Education* Open University Press, Milton Keynes

Fullan M. (1987) 'Managing Educational Change' in Preedy M. (ed.) *Approaches to Curriculum Management* Open University Press, Milton Keynes

Haynes F. (1988) *The Ethical School: Consequences, Consistency and Caring* Routledge, London

Hodgkinson (1999) 'The Triumph of the Will' in Begley P. and Leonard P. (eds) *The Values of Educational Administration* RoutledgeFalmer, London

Lafleur C. (1999) 'The Meaning of Time: Revisiting Values and Education Administration' in Begley P. and Leonard P. (eds) *The Values of Educational Administration* Falmer, London

Purvis J (1984) 'Women and Education: a Historical Account' in Dawtrey L., Holland J., Hammer M. and Sheldon S. (eds) *Equality and Inequality in Education Policy* Open University Press, Buckingham

Williams A.P.O. and Dobson P. (1997) 'Personnel Selection and Corporate Strategy' in Herriot P. and Anderson N. (eds) *International Handbook of Selection and Assessment* John Wiley, Chichester

Epilogue: Reflections on a year in the life of . . .

Forgotten

The day will come when you'll forget
    That you and I have ever met;
    Perhaps another name will be
    More precious to your memory –
When Summer suns at last have gone
    And Winter blasts are raging on.

Some day you will have ceased to pen
    A cheery letter now and then,
    To one who is far out of mind
Since love has lost its power to bind
When Summer suns at last have gone
    And Winter blasts are raging on.

Perhaps your eyes one day will be
    Wet with tears of sympathy –
When thinking how you once forgot
The one who wrote this tommy-rot;
When Summer suns at last have gone
    And Winter blasts are raging on.

Some day the blasts will rage and roar
    But they will speak to me no more –
    When I'm concealed in baser clay,
    And you'll remember how the day
    Of Summer memories were gone
And Winter blasts are raging on.

A. Fletcher

Why do we work? At the start of the diary I referred to the hermit looking down on a busy world wondering what people were doing and what its purpose was. For those of us who have spent our professional lives in schools, this is something to consider.

I once witnessed a scene where a teacher was berating a child because he had failed to underline the title to his essay. She was very cross with him and spoke sharply to him. She said that he needed to 'get his act together', otherwise he was 'doomed to fail'. Most of us have heard of (or possibly been) those teachers who, with the best intentions, want the students in their care to do their best and to achieve. The standards we set in our schools are, of course, very important but do the details matter so much?

Why did I set out to be a deputy head and is it the job I thought it would be? Education is the greatest gift that society can confer on the next generation. Education is what liberates us from our circumstances; it sets us free from the determination of wealth, social class and the generations. With education, the lowliest can become great; everyone has a personal worth and education can bring the realisation of that potential. But potential isn't enough. Without a determination to succeed potential is wasted and society remains static. Without ambition, our world perpetuates its inadequacies and injustices. Education is the potent force that makes all of our futures.

As a class teacher, I was able to convey the joy of Mathematics to those in my charge. I wanted to share the wonder of algebra and the potency of geometry. For me, teaching Mathematics in all its forms was the chance to share this world with others and create in them the means to achieve their own goals. As head of department, I was able to create and sustain the subject for many rather than the few. My work was about seeing the subject come alive for the whole school.

Being a deputy head is in one sense about taking the step towards headship. But in a very real way, it is about being part of a leadership team that can bring about real change and can create life chances for an entire school community. This final piece in this book contains some reflections on a year as the deputy headteacher.

Wanting to get it right and getting it wrong

I think we all want to get things right; we don't set out with the intention of getting them wrong. In my early days as deputy head I wanted to make a positive impression on the staff, my senior colleagues and the students. Moreover, when people came to me to ask 'what to do' or 'what I thought' I really wanted to be able to provide the answers. I didn't like it when I couldn't, and was left feeling deskilled. However, I came to realise that my core purpose is not to provide the answers, but to help colleagues find their own answers. There are many ways in which the job of deputy head differs from that of middle manager, but the main one is how public any errors become. Because so much of the work involves organising year groups, sometimes the whole school, because there is a lot to do and the volume of work is considerable, then the potential for disaster is so much greater.

I was discussing this with a fellow deputy Phillip, and he told me of the time when he had invited all the local primary schools for a matinee performance of his school's musical production. It was to be a nice occasion. The performers would benefit from a dress rehearsal in front of an audience and some much-needed primary liaison would be undertaken. He had invited 600 children from the feeder primary schools with their teachers. Buses had been organised to bring these children to the school for 1.30pm and all was set for an enjoyable afternoon. He had made arrangements with the site staff for chairs to be set out in the hall and refreshments to be available and all was in place. Phillip went to the school hall at 1.20pm to check that all was ready and thought that there weren't enough chairs. He went to find the site manager who said 450 chairs were set out, the maximum number the hall could hold! What this story illustrates is that we can spend a good deal of time organising events and processes and miss a small but significant detail. Phillip felt the ignominy of this organisational nightmare much more keenly because he felt foolish and had made such a basic and fundamental error.

It is part of the initiation into any organisation to learn to work effectively with the people around us. You may have a real sense of fear of the job itself. During the course of my first day as deputy head I was given a whole range of tasks and I felt that I couldn't do any of them. There were two aspects to this: the feeling that there was just so much to do (in that the volume of work was considerable and I had no control over the rate of input), and the feeling that the tasks themselves needed new skills or the different application of old ones. In those first days of feeling deskilled, I had to learn to apply my old skills to new situations. One of my jobs was the Form 7 return. I knew that this return existed and what it was for. I knew that it was important, but I didn't know what information it contained and being given it as a task to manage caused me some concern.

But these times are important because we can look back on them with wry amusement and some humility. In a sense, after a year I feel less competent to do the job than I did before I started. Being so heavily involved in the running of the school, I have learnt that my role is less about task management and more about people management. After a year I have realised the enormity of the task and indeed the complexity of the role I have. However, I am confident in my ability to do it and this seems to have been the major shift. Several events helped me to grow in confidence.

Things that have gone well

About a month into the post the headteacher and I started to think about the school development plan and what followed was to shape much of the way in which we work together. At the end of each day, we meet for a cup of coffee and a biscuit. The time of these meetings varies, as does their duration, depending on what other meetings we have been attending, our individual workloads or whatever. We discuss the events of the day and inform one another of the various happenings. This is a very important part of the way in which we lead the school, because it means that we both know all that has happened. It helps us a lot, meaning that we can respond as one, and there are few surprises.

At one of these evening meetings we started to discuss our aims over the next three years. We talked for about two hours on this subject and I went home, wrote up the meeting and presented it the next day to the head. What followed from this initial meeting was a raft of proposals that are to shape the school over the next three years at least. We discussed how we would consult with the staff, how we would measure our performance, and how the plan would be brought to life. This was a pivotal moment in my transition from subject leader to school leader because I was challenged in my thinking and had to think about what was needed for our school. In many ways, the work that went into the school development plan was part of the induction process, one outcome being the appreciation of it being 'our' school, that I was part of it.

One event that followed from this initial meeting was the staff meeting where we evaluated our progress since our OfSTED inspection and drew up a set of aims and objectives for the school development plan. This was an important meeting for me, not only because it was part of a process that would shape our school over the next year at least, but also because it was the first such meeting I led in the head's absence. The first time the head was out of school (albeit for about one hour) I felt the responsibility of the organi-sation. I now realise that the responsibility is not mine alone, there is a senior team and all my colleagues – but that first time, the responsibility felt great and solely mine. The senior team organised the meeting and all I had to do was to start it off and conclude it. But the fact that I was able to present the outcomes of the meeting to the head on his return strengthened our partnership and we both grew in confidence in one another.

Recruiting staff is a very important part of the job and it has to be right. In the first few months of my post, we recruited several key personnel. During this time a further transformation in my thinking took place. Until this point, all the recruitment decisions I had made had been confined to my subject expertise. My role as subject leader was to comment on a person's suitability as a subject teacher and to express my preference for an appointment. As deputy head, I was involved in drawing up the job description, the person specifi-cation, the advertisement, shortlisting, interview arrangements, panel interviews and final interviews. This process encouraged me to think about what kind of people we wanted in our school. What profile would they have, and how could we find this out? Many people find it hard to disagree with the boss – it isn't easy to express a different opinion – but the deputy has to be one person who is capable of saying exactly what he or she thinks. During these recruitment processes I was asked a number of times for my opinion. The head wasn't asking me whether I agreed with him; he was asking for my opinion. And if we disagreed, then we had to explore our differences and resolve them. Disagreeing about any matter is not a problem, but if you lack the courage to disagree then you shouldn't be a school leader. This is not because there has to be someone to check the power that runs the school, but because in order to make the right decisions for the organisation, agreement has to be meaningful. Part of being a school leader is the ability to think of things that the others haven't considered. An important step is to recognise that others can do some thinking for you.

This is the area that has caused me most reflection. When the job is demanding, when the agenda is full, it is easy to regard people in the organisation as part of the tactics. But as we become absorbed into the organisation, maturity brings recognition that the people are the strategy and that they are more important than the tasks themselves. The task culture is only realised through the people themselves. We learn to consult people not just to secure their commitment to doing the task, not just because it's the 'right' thing to do and means that a meeting will run more smoothly and you can say that you have 'consulted'. More significantly, we talk to people because they are fundamental to the organisation and we want them to be part of what is being attempted. This presupposes the confidence to let go and to trust in others.

Doing things the second time around

The prospect of doing things again is not one I normally relish, but now I feel differently. Having spent a year learning about the school through the tasks I have undertaken, I am now able to use this understanding to better effect.

Often, all we lack is experience and our opportunities to gain it are at their greatest during the first year in a new post in a new school. There are hard lessons to learn and sometimes the things that we have to do are not pleasant, but as deputy head you have the means to make a difference.

There have been two situations involving children that have made me think about this aspect of my work.

The first time was when I received a phone call from a parent complaining that her son was being bullied. She told me of an occasion where the boy had been ridiculed by another boy and some of his friends. She said that this had been going on for years (the boy was in Year 7) and she wanted it stopped. The parents wanted my personal guarantee that their son would be safe at school. This was one of those times when the responsibility for the school sits squarely on our shoulders; the parents didn't want a guarantee from the class teacher or even the head of year. It had to be from either the headteacher or me. Of course, no one can guarantee a child's safety but we did what we could and this involved elaborate arrangements where the boy was met and accompanied about the school (a gesture that was entirely over-whelming under the circumstances). I sent for the boy who was at the centre of the accusations and he gave me his story. I sent for the children who had been in his presence and they each gave me their story and added several names to my list of witnesses. Before long the number of children involved numbered around twenty-five and it became very difficult to see exactly what had happened to provoke this situation. I spent the next few days interviewing students to find out what had happened. I invited the parents for a meeting. They had taken matters into their own hands and had been to visit the aggressor's parents (who lived in the same village) and things had become unpleasant. The whole thing had started in primary school and continued when the children transferred to secondary school. It seemed very deep-seated. In fact no one could remember why the unpleasantness had started. But it was making the child very unhappy and his parents were naturally anxious for his welfare. I resolved the matter at this stage by telling all the children that I wasn't sure what had happened, but that it stopped from this moment on and that any further incidents would result in 'serious consequences'. So secret is the world of bullies and their victims that I don't know if my actions resolved the matter. But the bullying in school has stopped to my knowledge. I'm very glad that my actions meant that the unhappiness experienced by this child was recognised and some way was found to resolve the situation. When I see the boy around school, he doesn't look very different; his parents' gratitude was expressed in a 'Well, it'll be good if it works' kind of way. The child doing the bullying and his parents certainly found the episode unpleasant. But if my actions have made things better, then that's good. But only time will tell and I may never know whether what I did was right.

So what did I learn from this investigation? The first was that things are rarely one-sided. There is often another side to a comparatively simple story. Investigating these sorts of things takes time and although deputies are not rich in this resource, they can devote a whole day to them in a way that a classroom teacher cannot. Secondly, when parents contact the headteacher, they call on that person because they believe that things will be done, and of course they are right to assume this. But with that belief there is a need for the school to respond and be seen to respond. Thirdly, in these situations the victim's parents want the bully punished, and frequently they will want a child punished very severely. It is difficult to tell people in this highly emotional state that all that their child had told them isn't necessarily the case. How do we tell parents that their son in all his distress has brought some of this on himself? Fourthly, how do we tell parents that their child is a bully and all that goes with it? Fifthly, in the world of children there are many scuffles and fallings-out and as soon as adults are involved the stakes are raised. But as deputy head I was the one who had to say all these things, and live with the uncertainty that accompanies a situation complicated by years of unpleasantness and rancour.

The second occasion was when I excluded a child for a fixed term. The girl in Year 11 had been extremely rude to one of her teachers and made some sexual reference about him. This was not an isolated incident; several events had preceded this one. The headteacher was absent from school on the day in question, and so I was taking the decision to exclude the girl for a fixed term in his absence. The legal side of the exclusion process is clearly documented but I knew that the girl's parents could be extremely difficult.

Should I phone the head and ask for his agreement? Whenever the head is absent from school (and it is rare) I can always contact him, and there are certain circumstances in which I would not hesitate. If there was a major incident at school or if there was an issue involving the press – there are certain matters that only the head should and could handle, however long my experience. But an exclusion? I decided that I wouldn't contact him and telephoned the parents to ask them to come to school to collect their daughter because I was excluding her for three days. They agreed to the meeting and it was scheduled for 4pm. I had never had to tell parents of this decision before and I expected a difficult meeting. And it was. They didn't want their daughter to be excluded. The girl admitted that she was in the wrong and cried profusely. Referring to the other incidents, I said that as a school we needed to exact some punishment for the serious matters that were before us. However, having made clear my position and the fact that my decision was made, I changed tactic to talk about what would happen when the girl returned to school. My approach was to establish that on her return she would be under contract. This means the school, the parents and the child all agree to a range of things. For the child, this may be to co-operate in class, to complete classwork and homework on time and the like; for the parents, it may be to sign the contract daily or to reward the child. Our contract with this girl included convening a careers interview and organising a work schedule to help her get up to date with her coursework. The meeting turned from being antagonistic to being co-operative and positive. I won't say that they left the meeting happy. After all, their daughter was still to be excluded for three days, but they did all smile before they left. Saying the necessary words is never easy, but the outcome of the meeting was a positive resolution of the issues.

So what did I learn from this incident? Firstly, that I had to be resolute in the path I had chosen. After seeing all the tears and the girl's admission of her wrongdoing, it would have been easy to lose sight of the need for justice. But there had to be a punishment to restore the position. In the face of aggressive and articulate people, the position has to be firm. But this is not easy to do when it is two against one. But the school has to stand up for itself and, as the deputy head (acting in this case as the head), I am the one who has to defend its position. If I don't, who will? Secondly, having established the wrongdoing and having focused on the act rather than the person, I was able to move on. It is easy to denigrate a person but, as I wrote earlier in the book, we always have to remember that children in schools have parents who love them and we must recognise this in our dealings with them all. Thirdly, because I wasn't the person who had been subjected to the abuse, I was able to exercise some detachment from the incident and this is so important. When the teacher reported the incident to me, he was livid and wanted action. He wanted the girl permanently excluded. But as the deputy I had to exercise judgement and act in a proper manner which both left the child's dignity intact and reassured the teacher's demand for justice to have been seen to be done. This judgement is a fine balancing act that can go wrong with disastrous results. Fourthly, on this occasion I turned the meeting around. I thought 'win-win' and that was achieved. But things may not always end so happily. And, of course, if the contract hadn't worked when the girl came back to school, things would have been much harder the next time around. This may sound naïve because pupils with behaviour problems are often not susceptible to very much in the way of behaviour modification. The process I went through is win-win in another respect: if it works, then great; if it doesn't, then the correct steps have been taken to support the child. By and large (if it hadn't worked) this experience would have made the next meeting easier, not more difficult.

This is the risk that brings the greatest reward.

And of course there will be a next time.

However, the difficulties of resolving incidents involving children and their parents pale into insignificance compared to those involving teachers. Telling people that their teaching is unsatisfactory is awful but telling them that the matter will be referred to the headteacher (with all that it implies) is worse. I don't know if Jem was ever a good Spanish teacher, but Malcolm, the head of Department, certainly didn't think so. Setting up a process of lesson observations and targets was easy. Malcolm probably thought that doing so would make Jem improve. I asked Malcolm to hold weekly meetings with Jem to talk to her about the lessons she was delivering and to set targets that she could meet. As time passed when I talked to Malcolm he was very dismissive of Jem. He began to see her as a liability and as someone who caused him a lot of extra work. Jem never referred any disciplinary problems to him, but Malcolm knew that she had considerable difficulties in class control. Malcolm went to see Jem teach a Year 9 class and we held a meeting to discuss how the lesson had gone. I met Malcolm just before the meeting with Jem and he told me that the lesson was unsatisfactory, but that he couldn't say this. He was nervous of doing so because he knew that if he did it would change his relationship with Jem and he wasn't ready to do so. I think Malcolm found being a friend, a colleague and the line manager confusing. He had a real sense of role conflict. In the subsequent meeting I told Jem that the lesson was unsatisfactory.

In the ensuing months that led up to the disciplinary hearing where Jem was dismissed for incompetence, Malcolm never once told Jem that her lesson was unsatisfactory. He became more determined as time went on; he lost patience with her and he turned from being supportive to being aggressive.

What did I learn from this? Firstly, that when there are unpleasant things to say, often it is I who will have to say them. The deputy cannot hide behind any collegiality because we have to represent the interests of the children. Our first duty is to them. Secondly, in matters of competence, there comes a time when the subject leader (in this case) crosses the line. They have to decide where their loyalty lies. In this case Malcolm sided with me but it caused him distress and he needed a good deal of support. Thirdly, the head was to be distant from proceedings. This is the mode in which we operate but it would not be everyone's choice. In this situation, however, it means that these difficult matters can be referred to the head after due process, and the authority of the deputy, both as the head's agent and in his or her own right, is strengthened. The mutual trust between the head and deputy in these situations has to be total. The deputy is the representative of the head in so many ways and this is difficult. It creates a divide between the staff and the leadership team because the power resides with the leadership team who have the authority to separate staff from their jobs. Fourthly, now that Jem has gone the Spanish department has moved on and never speaks of her. They are glad she has left their department. No one will ever say that they are grateful for what we did, but at least they know that we did everything right and that this failing teacher wasn't allowed to continue to wreck the educational opportunities we try so hard to provide.

It is worth reflecting on these difficult occasions and thinking through what we learn from them. We learn things about ourselves when we have to do difficult things. Confronting children and adults about their failings and wrongdoings is never easy. The unpredictable nature of reactions makes for some anxiety about the outcomes. But when we have said these things once, we know we can say them again. Moreover, we learn that we can do these things, not only because they have to be done, but also because it is right to do so. Justice for wrongdoing is important to enact because a school leader represents the integrity and values of the school. The deputy's representation is, of course, secondary to the head's. The headteacher embodies the school's principles and values. But as deputy, you have to accord with these values and be that principle-centred leader.

Macbeath and Myers (1999) write that the quality of leadership in a school is tested most stringently by the nature and experience of a school's day-to-day life. It is the dynamic and perpetual nature of school life that excites and challenges school leaders to make things better.

As deputy head, I believe that what I do makes a difference. Sometimes things don't work the way I want them to and other times they work out far better than I could possibly have hoped. But the focus of my activity is the people in the organisation rather than the organisation itself. That is the most important lesson of all.

References

Fletcher A. (1897–1969) 'Forgotten', unpublished poem.
Macbeath J. and Myers K. (1999) *Effective School Leaders* Pearson
  Education, London